THE
VIRAL
VIDEO
MANIFESTO

THE VIRAL VIDEO MANIFESTO

WHY EVERYTHING YOU KNOW IS WRONG AND HOW TO DO WHAT REALLY WORKS

STEPHEN VOLTZ AND **FRITZ GROBE**

New York Chicago San Francisco Lisbon London Madrid Mexico City
Milan New Delhi San Juan Seoul Singapore Sydney Toronto

The *McGraw·Hill* Companies

1 2 3 4 5 6 7 8 9 0   DOC/DOC   1 8 7 6 5 4 3 2

ISBN 978-0-07-180338-0
MHID 0-07-180338-6

e-ISBN 978-0-07-180339-7
e-MHID 0-07-180339-4

All illustrations by Christopher Peterson, www.petersonland.com.

McGraw-Hill books are available at special quantity discounts to use as premiums and sales promotions or for use in corporate training programs. To contact a representative, please e-mail us at bulksales@mcgraw-hill.com.

This book is printed on acid-free paper.

Contents

INTRODUCTION
Creating a Virus

On a quiet Saturday morning in June 2006, we posted a three-minute video online. It showed the two of us, in the woods of Maine, wearing lab coats and safety goggles, dropping 500 Mentos mints into 100 bottles of Diet Coke creating a miniature Bellagio fountain show with geysers of soda.

We told just one person. But by that afternoon, 4,000 people had seen the video. By that night, 14,000.

On Monday morning, the *Late Show with David Letterman* called.

The next day, *Late Night with Conan O'Brien* called. The day after that, we were on NPR's *All Things Considered.* By the end of the week, the people who had built the *actual* Bellagio Fountains got in touch.

Seven months later, *Advertising Age* called that video "the most important commercial content of 2006." In 2009, it was voted the "Game Changer of the Decade" on GoViral.com.

All told, over 100 million people have now seen that video. All from telling just one person.

Almost every year since then, we've posted another video exploring how ordinary objects can do extraordinary things. Each one has gone viral and has received millions of views.

As we've made those videos, and as we've watched countless other videos go viral online, we've tried to distill what works and what doesn't. We've looked hard at why most attempts at viral video fail, and we've examined what makes the few that succeed so contagious.

This book is about what we've learned.

What This Book Isn't

In this book we won't tell you what camera to use or how to get the best sound and lighting.

We won't tell you how to upload your videos to YouTube, pick the right thumbnail, or work the system for maximum views.

We won't tell you how to build a following online through consistent content releases, dialogue with your audience, or other social media management techniques.

There is plenty of information out there about that stuff, and if the objective is to go viral, those tactics don't get at the heart of the matter. At the heart, it's the content itself that makes or breaks a viral video. This book is about that.

What This Book Is

This book is a style guide, a look at the overarching principles for how you can create videos that are built to go viral.

What makes videos go viral? It's not magic. We'll break down the common traits of successful online videos and show you how you can produce videos with those same viral characteristics.

Online video is something new, and the video techniques of the past just don't work. We'll look at the techniques we've found that *do* work.

We'll look at how you can learn to make videos that get people telling their friends, "You have got to see this!"

How to Watch the Videos as You Read

While we've tried to write for readers who don't have immediate access to the videos we discuss, if you can, we encourage you to watch the videos as you read. Here are two ways you can do that easily.

1. **Use a QR reader on your smartphone:** We've put Quick Response Codes (commonly known as QR Codes) in the margin whenever we discuss a video at some length and we think you might want to watch it at that point.

Using a QR reader app, just point your smartphone at the QR Code in the margin, and the corresponding video will load onto your phone automatically. QR readers are easy to use with almost any smartphone or iPod touch. If you're not sure which one to use, we've got links to a couple QR readers we like at ViralVideoManifesto.com.

An Example of a QR Code

2. **Visit ViralVideoManifesto.com:** If you want to watch online with a web browser—or if you want to watch every video we mention even in passing—we've collected links to all of the videos and organized them by chapter at ViralVideoManifesto.com, so you can easily watch them in the order in which you'll encounter them as you read. To the right is a QR Code that'll take you to that list.

ViralVideo Manifesto .com

The Four Chapters for Marketers

This book isn't just for marketers. It's for everyone who is interested in what makes video go viral.

With more and more people skipping ads both on television and online, however, viral video has become an important tool of brand marketers. And if you're looking to make a viral video for your brand, you have to deal with issues that other viral video creators don't.

In the four "For Marketers" chapters in this book, we'll look at how certain traditional advertising methods can get in your way online, and we'll spell out the steps you can take to create viral ads that people want to watch. If you're not concerned with using viral video for marketing your brand, feel free to skip over these chapters.

STEPHEN VOLTZ
FRITZ GROBE
Buckfield, Maine
November 2012

THE

VIRAL
VIDEO
MANIFESTO

CHAPTER 1

Everything You Know Is Wrong

Most of what we all know about creating compelling video simply doesn't apply to viral video. Why not? Because what works in television does not work online. As Tim Street, vice president of mobile video at mDialog and creator of the viral video series *French Maid TV*, says, one of the problems with today's online content is that "we're taking things that look like a TV show or look like movies and putting them on the Internet."

Television is designed primarily to hook and hold viewers because, on television, as soon as the viewer flips the channel, the game is lost. So for 60 years, television has been getting better and better at keeping us from changing the channel—no matter what.

The production and editing techniques developed for television— quick cuts, multicamera shoots, odd camera angles, dolly shots, crane shots, news crawls at the bottom of the screen, and the like—do that beautifully. Over the years, television producers have developed a style that taps into the primitive, instinctive parts of our brains to hold our attention continuously, *whether or not the content itself is compelling.*

If you've ever seen a TV news reporter in a trench coat urgently "reporting live" from in front of a dark, deserted courthouse at 11:15 at night with a news crawl at the bottom of the screen alerting you that a "WINTER STORM MAY BE HEADING TO AREA," you know what we mean.

Television grabs us and keeps us watching for hours at a time so that, at the end of the day, even if we're drained and unsatisfied, television has done what it needs to do to be profitable: it has delivered our eyeballs to its advertisers.

But to go viral online, if all you do is hold our attention, you've failed.

In viral video, your job isn't to keep viewers from changing the channel. It's to get them to love what you've made so much that they want to stop what they're doing and tell their friends.

Viral video is about sharing.

That makes it different from every other kind of moving picture ever made.

From *David After Dentist* to *Evolution of Dance*, this new kind of video doesn't use cuts, creative camera angles, or other tricks to keep us passively watching. These videos have gotten millions of people actively excited, to the point where they have passed those videos on to millions of their friends with the message, "You've got to see this."

David After Dentist   Evolution of Dance

So how do you make that happen? How do you get people to share?

You can't force it, so there are no guarantees. But that doesn't mean there is no rhyme or reason. There are certain traits that viral videos have in common—traits that help make them *contagious*. And that's something you can control. You can make a video with contagious qualities.

Some viruses will be extremely contagious within a small group of people—90-minute videos of experts playing video games will spread like crazy in certain circles. Other viruses may be less intensely contagious, but they will infect vast numbers of people—

Charlie Bit My Finger– Again!

Charlie Bit My Finger—Again! has been seen over 460 million times. You might have been able to fend off catching it until everyone you knew had watched it, but eventually most of us finally gave in.

Just as we do with infectious diseases, we build up resistance to some kinds of viral content but not others. *Coke & Mentos* is like an influenza that swept the world, and it has settled into a constant level of infection with recurring flu seasons.

And like the common cold, there is no known cure for *LOLCats*. It will always be there.

To get at what traits make these things contagious, let's look at sharing in general. Word of mouth has always been powerful, and the Internet has given everyone a megaphone. Whether you're on YouTube, Facebook, Twitter, Pinterest, or the next new social network, the way things spread is the same. Understanding

The Extreme Diet Coke & Mentos Experiments

LOLCats

the mechanisms of sharing will continue to be crucial to creating successful online content, whatever the next trend may be.

Sharing is about emotion. Researchers Jonah Berger and Katherine Milkman at the Wharton School, University of Pennsylvania, have studied why people share online, and they have found two key insights:

▸ We're more likely to share something that makes us feel good.
▸ We're more likely to share something that gets us fired up.

So negative emotions like sadness that make us passive are the worst because when we're down, we don't want to share. We just want to be left alone. Passive, positive emotions like contentment still don't stimulate sharing because, well, we're content.

Negative emotions like anger and fear make us more active, so we're more likely to tell people about what's making us ticked off or afraid than what's making us sad.

Best of all, however, are the things that are both exciting and positive—the stuff that gets us saying, "That was hysterical!" or "That was amazing!" To get people sharing, you need to get them actively engaged with strong, positive emotions.

And here is where the attention-holding tricks of television not only don't help but actually work against you. While edits, pans, zooms, and sound effects will get and hold our attention, they do so at a cost. Research by Robert Kubey at Rutgers, Mihaly Csikszentmihalyi at Claremont, and others has shown that these techniques make viewers more passive and they distract viewers from the content itself.

Many of the techniques used in television exploit a primal human reaction known as the *orienting response*, which is a reflexive reaction triggered when we see a sudden movement or hear a sudden noise. The orienting response makes us immediately turn our attention to the source of the sound or movement. That's a crucial reflex to have if there may be a tiger hiding in the jungle or a cobra lurking in the grass. But it can also be exploited.

Like a sudden movement above us in the trees, those TV edits, pans, zooms, and sound effects also trigger our orienting response. Our brains immediately need to know, "What was that movement? What was that sound?" It's a sure way to get our attention. And on television, these little reflex triggers are often coming at us several times per second, so our orienting response will not let us turn away. And that's when we pay a cost.

Stimulating the orienting response like that has some side effects. Our heart rates slow. The alpha waves in our brains are blocked for a few seconds. TV viewers studied by Kubey and Csikszentmihalyi reported feeling relaxed and passive, and that passivity continued after they switched off the TV. Passivity is exactly what you want if you don't want viewers to change the channel. As Kubey and Csikszentmihalyi point out, on television, "viewing begets more viewing." Putting your audience in a passive mood is a problem, however, when your goal is to get viewers to take the active step of telling their friends about what they've just seen.

To go viral, you have to get your audience actively engaged, not passively watching. Television techniques that make us lethargic and passive work directly against that.

We humans also have, unfortunately, limited mental resources, and if you trigger our orienting response, our involuntary, "What was that?" reaction depletes some of those limited mental resources. Though you will have successfully gotten our attention, researchers like Annie Lang at Indiana University have shown that you've also reduced the mental resources we have available to process everything else we're taking in.

In other words, the edits, the zooms, and the sound effects that draw our attention also increase the load on our brains and slightly but significantly pull our attention away from the heart of your content and focus us instead on the attention-grabbing tricks.

So while TV is a master at demanding our attention and holding onto it, television also makes us passive and distracts us from the actual content, making it more difficult to create an emotional connection.

This research fits with what we see out in the trenches of viral video.

It's only when you get rid of all the old TV tricks and, instead, you really connect with us and get us fired up and smiling, that we'll stop and tell our friends about the cool online video we just saw.

If you want to create that emotional connection that leads to sharing, there are four core principles that we've found are crucial for you to understand:

1. Be true.
2. Don't waste our time.
3. Be unforgettable.
4. Ultimately, it's all about humanity.

These four principles will help you make your video contagious.

The more you can stick to all four, the better, although you don't have to be perfect to create a contagious video. Strength in one area can often overcome a deficiency in another.

Throughout this book, we'll discuss how a number of online videos have used these principles to go viral and what happens when video producers ignore them. And you'll see how, if you shoot for all four, you can start an epidemic.

⊙ A Word About View Counts

Throughout this book, we generally use view counts as a proxy for contagiousness, so the first time we mention a video, we note the YouTube view count for the most popular copy as of the time we went to press. Sometimes, there are many copies with significant views or there was a copy with even more views that was taken down, so in a few instances, the number we list is only part of the picture.

View counts are the best measure we have right now for assessing contagiousness, but use them with caution. They're only a rough approximation because contagiousness is just one factor in the view count equation. Celebrity and money can also boost view counts.

Celebrity backing alone can shoot a video from obscurity to online hit in a matter of days. Paul Vasques, for example, posted his loopy *Yosemitebear Mountain Giant Double Rainbow 1-8-10* video online in January 2010 where it sat unwatched for six months without getting any traction.

Double Rainbow

Then Jimmy Kimmel tweeted about it, and view counts skyrocketed. Today, thanks to Kimmel, *Double Rainbow* has had 34 million views.

View counts can also be pumped up with an ad buy or social media spend. Using view counts alone, it's hard to compare the contagiousness of something like *Evolution of Dance*, which had no promotional budget, with something like Volkswagen's *The Force* or Old Spice's *The Man Your Man Could Smell Like*, both of which had the benefit of major marketing pushes.

And views can simply be bought. To test this, in February 2012, *Los Angeles Times* reporters David Sarno and Jack Leonard paid two online video promotion companies a total of $103 to generate views for a video of the most boring thing they could think of: paint drying. That $103 bought

Blue Streek 022012

Sarno and Leonard's *Blue Streek 022012* over 60,000 views. Some of those views were at a British yoga site. Others were on a site registered in Mongolia.

We can only guess at how much promotional budgets, celebrity involvement, and view buying have affected the view counts of the videos we discuss in this book, but whether there was promotion behind them or not, we have chosen the videos we discuss here because we believe that they have the traits of contagious content. Just remember to take view counts, especially of videos from major players, with a grain of salt.

CHAPTER 2

The Most Important Idea in This Book

Viral video is the twenty-first-century sideshow.

Before we started making viral videos, our expertise was in theatrical circus. Stephen had a one-man show. Fritz was a world-record-setting juggler, and he toured with a Cirque du Soleil spinoff. Between the two of us, we've spent decades examining the fundamental principles of this type of performance and putting them into action.

Somewhat to our surprise, what we have found in viral video is that many of the same rules apply. This is vaudeville. This is street performing. This is the sideshow for our times.

Traditionally, the *sideshow*, sometimes called the "ten-in-one," consisted of ten different acts under one tent. It was a combination of skill acts (like the jugglers, the magicians, and the escape artists); danger acts (like the fire eaters, the sword swallowers, and the knife throwers); and the oddities (like the bearded ladies, the contortionists, and the two-headed turtles). Each gave the audience something new, amazing, or downright weird to marvel and often gawk at. The sideshow was in your face, with a gritty reality filled with wild things you'd never seen before.

That's what we see today in viral video. It's immediate and unpolished, and it embraces the bold, daring, and unabashedly strange.

You might think of this kind of performing as low or artless, but there can be a great deal of careful crafting involved, and like viral video, it can range from the bizarre to the beautiful.

Whether it's a guy hammering a nail into his nostril or a Cirque du Soleil aerial ballet, video of a sneezing baby panda or Susan Boyle singing, the core of what makes them work is the same.

A key element of the sideshow is the up-close, raw, unfiltered experience of actually seeing things like a guy doing a backflip into a pair of jeans. It is real. You saw it. You were there. That's the core of our Rule One for viral video: **Be true.**

If you are a street performer or a carnival barker, your living depends on people stopping what they're doing and watching you instead of walking away. You learn very quickly to cut everything from your act that doesn't hold people's attention. Online, it's exactly the same. That gives us Rule Two: **Don't waste my time.**

And just like a sideshow act, every viral video has a hook—something new and remarkable that provokes the reaction "I've never seen that before."

So, "Step right up! Step right up! Watch a baby monkey riding backward on a pig!" "See what happens when we put an iPhone in a blender!" "Watch as a strange young man under a sheet sobs and screams, 'Leave Britney alone!'" "See over 100 bottles of Coke explode into the air!" These kinds of hooks are the basis for our Rule Three: **Be unforgettable.**

And finally, just like the sideshow, in the end, it comes down to Rule Four: **Ultimately, it's all about humanity.**

To create a strong, positive emotional experience, the people are what matter. The best circus and sideshow performers—and the best viral video creators—are the ones who have been able to project their humanity, to create a connection with the audience.

Be True

The guy swallowing swords, the guy eating
fire, the guy hammering a nail into his nose;
it hit me that these were not tricks.

—TODD ROBBINS, SIDESHOW PERFORMER

We crave true, authentic experiences. Television and movies give us prepackaged retellings of life—entertaining, but unreal. The Internet, on the other hand, can give us unfiltered reality as no other medium can. The kid whose brother bites his finger and the news reporter who falls out of a vat of grapes: these are real. They're true. And that truth helps make them contagious.

The most contagious online content provokes strong, active, positive emotions. Being true helps create and turn up the volume on that emotional connection.

At its best, this twenty-first-century sideshow keeps it raw. From a sword swallower to a bed of nails, part of the power is that we are witnessing this with our own eyes, that it's undeniably real.

Videos that are true create this same direct, personal connection between the creator and the audience. These videos are not made by actors, not by editors, not by camerapeople with film school camera moves. These are videos that are made by real people, for real people.

Everything that interferes with that personal connection reduces the chance that we'll share with our friends. Staying true keeps the emotional connection strong and makes it more contagious.

So here is your opportunity with online video: make us a fly on the wall. No actors, no edits, no fancy camerawork. Just do what is necessary to be true, and no more.

Look at the top videos on YouTube, and time and time again you'll see proof of the power of being true:

- *Charlie Bit My Finger—Again!:* Yes, Charlie bit his finger. Again. 460 million views.
- *JK Wedding Entrance Dance:* Everyone dances down the aisle. 76 million views.

Links to These Examples

- *The Sneezing Baby Panda:* A baby panda and, yes, a sneeze. 140 million views.
- *Evolution of Dance:* A live dance performance. 200 million views.

The fact that these are real events and real people is part of what makes the videos contagious.

No Pretense, No Packaging

Take a look at *Greyson Chance Singing Paparazzi* (48 million views), a homemade amateur video of a 12-year-old playing the piano and singing the Lady Gaga song "Paparazzi" at his sixth-grade music festival. The camera shakes, sometimes a lot. The

Greyson Chance Singing Paparazzi

audio is only what the camera could pick up in the room. Some of the kids in the background are clearly enjoying the performance, while others look distractedly around the room.

Everything about it is true. The content is true, the way it was shot is true, and we feel that we are simply there in the room watching it happen.

That truth is the key to the emotional connection that this video creates: it's just a kid at a school concert, surrounded by other kids watching, and we're there with them. There's no pretense, no packaging.

Would a multicamera shoot with professional lighting, professional audio, and a perfect audience increase our emotional connection to the video? No. Polished, professional packaging would destroy the feeling this video creates of our being privileged to witness something that really happened. When we see actors, camerapeople, producers, or editors using the tools of their trade, we know we're getting something that's been repackaged and that knowledge sabotages contagiousness.

The video of Greyson Chance takes us there, as if we ourselves are sitting in that audience, enjoying something happening in front of our own eyes, and we can lean over and tell our friends: "This is amazing."

How does Greyson Chance stack up against Lady Gaga herself? Of all the YouTube videos of "Paparazzi," his simple, homemade video is second only in views to Lady Gaga's official version.

Keeping It Real

The standard practice in television is to control everything and make things perfect, and while TV audiences know that, it's such a baseline assumption that it's easy to forget. We notice TV's artificiality only when we compare it to real-life footage like *Charlie Bit My Finger—Again* or *Numa Numa*. To make a video that has a chance to go viral, you need to step back from the approach taken by television and make a video that is real.

You may be tempted to hire professional actors so that you get just the right reactions. Don't. Use real people.

You may think you'll do better if you dress it up and make everyone look great. Don't. Keep it real.

Your director may suggest that you make it "more interesting" with flashy camera moves. Don't. You want your audience to feel like they're right there at the sideshow, not at home watching television, so just capture the truth as it happens.

To make it more contagious, keep it true.

CHAPTER 3

Show Me Something Real

JK Wedding Entrance Dance

The easiest way to be true is to show us real people having real reactions to real events. What actually happens when you drop 500 Mentos mints into 100 bottles of Coke as we did in *The Extreme Diet Coke & Mentos Experiments*? What happens when you really send 250,000 superballs bouncing down a hill in San Francisco as Sony Bravia did in its *Balls* video (4.9 million views)? And what really happens behind the scenes on the TV news as we saw in *What News Anchors Do During Commercial Breaks* (3 million views)?

These aren't about actors and their craft. These are about real people.

These don't re-create anything. They capture the real thing when it really happened.

Links to These Examples

Show us the reality. Reality will help you forge that crucial emotional connection with your audience. When you show us real people and real events, your work has a chance to go viral in a way that scripted videos can never approach. To see how this works, let's look at two similar pieces: one real and one that was elaborately faked.

Celebrating a Real Moment

On June 2, 2009, Jill Peterson married Kevin Heinz at Christ Lutheran Church in St. Paul, Minnesota. When the wedding began, instead of Mendelssohn's traditional "Wedding March" playing as the ushers closed the doors for the ceremony to begin, Chris Brown's 2008 pop hit "Forever" began pumping out of speakers into the chapel. Then, instead of sedately walking to their places for the ceremony, the ushers tossed their wedding programs into the air and began to dance down the aisle as if they were in a nightclub, rocking out to the music. Then the doors opened and the bridesmaids, in red party dresses and identical sunglasses, danced their way in, matching each other step-for-choreographed-step, to the front. After the entire wedding party had entered this way, the groom came styling down the aisle, followed by the bride in her traditional wedding dress holding her bridal bouquet, with an unforgettable, joyful, dancing entrance.

JK Wedding Entrance Dance

Several weeks later, when Kevin uploaded the five-minute home video of this as *JK Wedding Entrance Dance*, it went viral almost immediately, amassing 10 million views in its first week. To date it has had some 76 million views. The video spawned viral spoofs like *JK Divorce Dance* (9.9 million views) and *The T-Mobile Royal Wedding* (26 million views). Television shows like *The Office* featured their own versions of the dance down the aisle. Jill and Kevin's video was such a huge hit that their little wedding in St. Paul, Minnesota, even put Chris Brown's "Forever" back on the charts at number 4 on iTunes and number 3 on Amazon.com.

That's the power that real people and real emotion can have online.

What Happens with Actors

Just a few days after Jill and Kevin got married in Minnesota, and even before *JK Wedding Entrance Dance* was online, the folks at Disney staged a fake wedding proposal at Disneyland, and on June 9, 2009, they posted a video of it on YouTube with this coyly misleading description: "A magical moment happens on Main Street, U.S.A., when a young man proposes to his girlfriend on a Summer evening in Disneyland® Resort."

Disneyland Musical Marriage Proposal

The video opens with what appears to be security camera footage of ordinary vacationers strolling along Disneyland's main drag. A young man with perfect hair steps away from his date, takes an orange megaphone out of a shopping bag, and begins to call out to the passersby: "Attention! Can I get everyone's attention please?"

As people stop to watch, he uses the megaphone to propose marriage to the young woman with him. Several apparent strangers join in with an elaborate song and dance number that builds up to popping the question. It's clear that at least some of the people in the crowd are ringers who have been well rehearsed, but the implication is that those folks are all part of the extravaganza arranged by the young man with the megaphone.

Why did Jill and Kevin's *JK Wedding Entrance Dance* get 76 million views, while Disney's similar, and in many ways more impressive, *Musical Marriage Proposal* get only 5.1 million?

Real vs. Fake

JK Wedding Entrance Dance is simple, real, and powerful. It's shot with one camera from a single location and the people in it, their hair, their clothes, their bodies, are real. The true emotion of that real moment is extremely contagious.

Disneyland Musical Marriage Proposal, on the other hand, is artificial. Clues hinting at its dishonesty are everywhere. While in many ways the folks at Disney did an admirable job of faking things, watching *JK Wedding Entrance Dance* and Disney's *Marriage Proposal* back-to-back, it's impossible not to feel the difference between real and fake immediately.

Disneyland Musical Marriage Proposal is overflowing with tip-offs that it's a fraud. From the very start, both lead actors are so shiny and well scrubbed that they look as though they just stepped out of a toothpaste commercial. The dialogue feels scripted, the sound quality is unusually good, the lighting is flawless, and somehow, while the video captures the action from more camera angles than we get in most primetime TV shows, not once does one camera catch a glimpse of another. How is that possible without doing multiple takes?

All in all there are dozens of subtle hints like these that we're watching a sham, and consciously or unconsciously, our brain takes them all in. Yet every one of the people involved with creating *Disneyland Musical Marriage Proposal* was a seasoned professional. Disney doesn't work with anything less. With all the talent, budget, rehearsal, and other resources that Disney brought to bear on that project, even they couldn't pull off what Jill and Kevin did with an hour and a half of rehearsal the day before their wedding: a video viewers instantly knew they could trust.

Viewers may not be able to articulate exactly why they don't trust *Disneyland Musical Marriage Proposal* and why they do trust *JK Wedding Entrance Dance*, but they can tell the difference instantly, and it's only the true one they want to pass on to their friends. That's why *JK Wedding Entrance Dance* got an order of magnitude more views than *Disneyland Musical Marriage Proposal*.

Make the Real Choice

So what should **you** do? On the one hand, you could try to fake reality more convincingly than Disney did. Some of the major flaws in *Disneyland Musical Marriage Proposal* could be fixed, and a few basic changes could help create a more convincing imitation of real life. For example, Disney's video could have been more contagious if it had been shot with less perfectly coiffed actors dressed in ordinary touristy T-shirts and shorts and recorded entirely on a single cell phone video camera. (We might also take out things like the giveaway "®" in "Disneyland® Resorts" in the YouTube description.)

But even then, after all that time, money, and effort, how close would that come to the true passion and joy of Jill and Kevin's simple wedding entrance dance that made their video a runaway viral hit?

Show us reality. If you want to show us a beautiful wedding proposal, show us a real one. Ditch the actors. Throw away the script. Show us someone who is in love and nervous and excited and is going to propose. For real.

It's not about the perfect camera angles or making sure no one flubs his or her lines. From *Greatest Marriage Proposal EVER!!!* (23 million views) to *Jamin's Downtown Disney Flashmob Proposal* (5.8 million views—and a *genuine* Disney proposal), the emotional power that makes these videos contagious comes from actual situations and authentic human reactions.

From *JK Wedding Entrance Dance* to Sony's *Balls* to other viral video hits like Matt Harding's *Where the Hell Is Matt? 2008* (43 million views), Austin Hall's *Daft Hands* (54 million views), and the classic *Will It Blend?* series from Blendtec (multiple videos with multiple millions of views), what works is what's real. Capturing real people doing real things is far more contagious that hiring actors to fake it.

We want to share experiences that are true. So, whether you find it or create it, show us something cool *that really happened* and you've got a chance to make us care enough to share with our friends. That's what "going viral" is all about.

⏵ *What About Videos That Try to Fake Us Out?*

Being true is a key part of forging a positive emotional connection with your audience, and that emotional connection helps make your video contagious.

But this is the twenty-first-century sideshow, and the sideshow also has a long tradition of trickery. Was the bearded lady wearing a fake beard? Was that really a mermaid skeleton, or was it just the body of a fish attached to a monkey's torso?

Online, we find fakes as well, from the *Cadbury Gorilla*, where either a gorilla or someone in a very convincing gorilla suit plays a professional drum solo, to *MEGAWOOSH*, where a guy in a wet suit shoots down a giant waterslide and appears to fly through the air an astonishingly long distance, landing perfectly in a wading pool full of water. These videos violate Rule One, Be True, so how does that affect their contagiousness?

First, there are the obvious fakes. *Rob Dyrdek on a Floating Skateboard???* tried to convince us that someone built a *Back-to-the-Future*-style hoverboard. The stunt was fake, the acting was bad, and this video stalled out at 660,000 views.

Then there are the good fakes, like the *Cadbury Gorilla*, *MEGAWOOSH*, and *Walk on Water (Liquid Mountaineering)*. Liquid Mountaineering's video tried to convince us that people were actually learning to run on water. While it sounded impossible, the well-made video made the

Cadbury Gorilla

MEGA-WOOSH

Floating Skate-board???

Walk on Water

idea seem just barely credible. Almost 12 million people watched, wondered, and argued whether or not it was real.

At their best, these out-and-out fakes are trying to have fun with us. Can you really run on water? Did Kobe Bryant really just jump over that moving car? (See *Laker Kobe Bryant Attempts Massive Stunt… And Succeeds! Real?* [5.2 million views]) Playing this "Is it real?" game can be fun.

Kobe
Bryant
Stunt

But when the objective is to create positive emotion, it's a dangerous game. Are we smiling at the end? Then we might still share the video. But more often than not, if we even suspect a video might be fake, we won't share it because we don't want to look dumb in front of our friends. We don't want them to say, "You didn't realize that was fake?!"

Remember, active, *positive* emotion is what makes us most likely to share. If you make us feel distrustful or if we just don't care because we think it's fake, we're negative or apathetic. Neither of those is likely to get us clicking on the share button.

If it does work, is it worth it? If you get millions of views, will it create the kind of relationship with your viewers that you want? That's for you to decide.

So the *Cadbury Gorilla* made us smile. We shared that one. David Beckham improbably kicking soccer balls into trash cans on the beach made us suspicious. We didn't share that one.

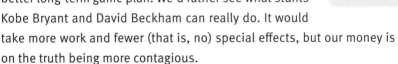

David
Beckham
Stunt

While fakery can work, we think that the truth is a better long-term game plan. We'd rather see what stunts Kobe Bryant and David Beckham can really do. It would take more work and fewer (that is, no) special effects, but our money is on the truth being more contagious.

Back in 1999, Tiger Woods made an ad for Nike in which he bounced a golf ball on the face of a golf club. One single, fixed camera, in one uninterrupted 24-second shot, showed Tiger Woods doing a seemingly impossible sequence of tricks: he kept the ball bouncing on the tiny

Tiger Woods Stunt

face of the club as he moved the club under his legs and behind his back, before finally popping the ball up in the air and then hitting it right out of the air and off into the distance.

And it was real. That's the best version of this game.

CHAPTER 4

Just Press Record and Do It

OK Go–Here It Goes Again

Viral video is about raw, unfiltered experience, so don't dress it up.

Every edit and camera move filters our experience and makes us feel more like we're watching a TV and less like we're actually there. You want us to feel like we're right there and that there are no barriers between us and what happened. As Trish Sie, the Grammy-winning choreographer behind several of OK Go's hit viral videos, has said, "[You] want to stick to that original feeling of: if you were in the room, this is what it really looked like."

It's no accident that many of the biggest viral videos of all time are unedited footage shot with a single, fixed camera with absolutely no edits. Viral hits like *The Sneezing Baby Panda, Numa Numa, Evolution of Dance*, and *Here It Goes Again* (OK Go's treadmill dance) were all captured in a single uninterrupted shot with a camera that never moved.

Conventional media professionals who have spent their lives working in television and film marvel at this as though it were an impediment, that these videos have miraculously succeeded in spite of their unprofessionally "low production values," when in fact, those techniques—shooting with a single fixed camera and keeping edits as minimal as possible—are actually a crucial part of *what makes them successful.*

In general, high production values, by which we mean the editing, camerawork, lighting, sound, costuming, sets, makeup, and related techniques of conventional movies and television, get in the way of the truth. Do online viewers care if *The Sneezing Baby Panda* was shot on high-end HD equipment or just on an old cell phone? Would *Evolution of Dance* have gotten more views if it had had the benefit of a professional lighting designer? Would *Here It Goes Again* have been better if the band had worn Vegas-style costumes? Not likely. Online, all we need is the truth.

Your task is only to make your video clear enough so that the truth comes through. We need to be able to see and hear the action. Any production techniques that don't directly contribute to that simple goal are unnecessary. And any unnecessary production techniques will get between you and your audience's raw, unfiltered experience.

Every pan and zoom, every edit, and every one of those all too alluring production techniques taught in film school creates a barrier between you and your audience. Every time you stimulate our orienting response, you are distracting us from your actual content, and it's your content that drives sharing. Every time you use a dolly or a crane shot, you're telling us that what we're seeing is not exactly what we would have seen if we had been right there with you at the time, but instead, it's been filtered and diluted.

Fight to keep it simple. Jumping to another camera angle may be eye-catching, but is it helping you be true?

Beware of the voice in your head that says, "It would look really cool if we put a camera over there... And over there... And over there..."

Give us the best seat in the house; then put the camera there and don't move it.

In viral video, the *best* approach is to just press record and do it.

A Guy, a Stage, and a Spotlight

In 2001, back in the days of dial-up modems and long before streaming video online was practical, motivational speaker Judson Laipply came up with a new idea for an ending to his "inspirational comedy" presentation. He would demonstrate the history of dance by mixing together 12 of the most popular dances from the past 50 years and performing them back-to-back in a short one-person dance mashup. It was a hit with his audiences.

Evolution
of Dance

For the next five years he kept refining it, learning new dance moves and adding them to the mashup. By 2006, he had incorporated 30 different dances, and he had matched them to a music track that included everything from Elvis Presley's "Hound Dog" and Chubby Checker's "The Twist" to Los del Rio's "Macarena" and on through to Jay-Z's "Dirt Off Your Shoulder" and 'N Sync's "Bye, Bye, Bye."

Then, in 2006, he videotaped it. He shot with one camera, in a single, static, unedited take. In frame is simply Laipply, wearing faded blue jeans and an orange T-shirt, standing on a dark stage and lit by a single spotlight. An announcer's voice comes over the PA system and says simply, "Evolution. Of Dance." Elvis Presley begins to play, and Laipply begins his crazy six-minute, one-man dance mashup.

On April 6, 2006, he posted the video online, and it immediately took off. By the end of the year it had an amazing 70 million views. As of this writing, *Evolution of Dance* has had over 200 million views, and it is one of the most popular viral videos of all time.

When Laipply appeared on *Oprah*, she marveled at how popular his video had become even though, as she put it, "it's just a guy, a stage, and a spotlight!" But in fact, it was exactly that simplicity that made us all feel like we were right there in the room with him when it happened. It was that simplicity that helped rocket him to Internet stardom.

If *Evolution of Dance* had been shot as a conventional music video with multiple cameras, odd angles, and quick MTV edits, it would have lost one of the keys to its contagiousness. All those production tricks would have just obscured the truth. *Evolution of Dance* is not packaged MTV perfection. That wouldn't be true. What's contagious is that Judson Laipply is a real guy, dancing his butt off in front of a live, pumped-up crowd. That raw, unfiltered experience is what makes his simple straightforward video so compelling.

So don't fall into the trap of making a video that relies on the conventional production techniques of film and television that mesmerize us. Instead, just point the camera at something compelling, press the record button, and give us something we'll want to share online.

Getting It Right on Take 72

One group that really understands the power of a single, fixed camera is the band OK Go and their choreographer Trish Sie. They have used the technique repeatedly, and they've shown time and again that this choice creates a direct, personal connection. It keeps things true.

The band's first video, *A Million Ways*, went viral back in 2005, just as streaming video was coming online. They had made a simple—but carefully practiced and beautifully performed—rehearsal video on

OK Go–
A Million
Ways

lead singer Damian Kulash's backyard patio, recording a dance Sie had choreographed that they wanted to perform as an encore at their concerts. They had shot the video with no intention of showing it to anyone else, and they made it only so that they could see for themselves what the dance looked like before they did it on stage.

Since their live audiences seemed to like the live dance number, the band wound up giving DVD copies of the video to various friends and fans, and before they knew it, it had appeared online and was going viral. *A Million Ways* ended up getting 500,000 views at a time when 500,000 video views was almost unheard of.

That viral success led to a feature on *All Things Considered,* where host Robert Siegel remarked on the video's unexpected popularity despite the fact that, as Siegel put it, "it's not the sort of video one would expect to see on cable music channels with lots of editing or special effects or fancy costumes. It is highly choreographed, but it's a single shot… and they're dancing on a backyard brick patio."

In fact, that homemade, backyard patio quality was key to getting *A Million Ways* to go viral.

When they first began planning out the video, Sie and OK Go already had a thorough understanding of the power that comes from shooting a video with a backyard, "just press record and do it" attitude. As Sie explains, "The work that I've done with OK Go and the work I've done with other people, I like to just have it be: You know what? You could have done this too in your garage. You could have done this in your park or your backyard or your living room." Not surprisingly then, when she choreographed *A Million Ways,* her approach was to find power in simplicity and truth, not in costume, showiness, or production tricks. The result was, as Damian Kulash (who is also Sie's younger brother) put it, "super-low-tech"—and according to the band's fans who passed it around online, an infectious video that went viral.

Sie and the band used the same approach in 2006 for their biggest viral success to date, their famous treadmill video for the song "Here It Goes Again" (there are multiple copies online, with 13 to 52 million views). This time, she choreographed an elaborate dance on eight moving treadmills, creating an

OK Go–
Treadmills

unforgettable video that won a Grammy and was named to *Time* magazine's list of the all-time best music videos.

And how did they shoot it? A single, fixed camera; no edits. It took 17 takes to get it right, and it was worth it. The video is immediate, powerful, and contagious.

After their smash success with the treadmill video, Trish Sie began thinking about what she wanted to do next with the band, and she asked herself what she would do if she was given the chance to make any kind of video she wanted. Her answer to herself was, "I want dogs dancing!" (a classic sideshow-style act). For several years she and the band mulled the idea, and in 2010 when the band was preparing to release its *Of the Blue Colour of the Sky* album, they were ready to try it.

And they knew exactly how they wanted to approach production.

The video for the song "White Knuckles" opens in silence with the four band members standing side by side, dressed completely in white. Behind them is a five-foot-tall pyramid of small, white, plastic Ikea trash baskets. When the music kicks in, more trash baskets are tossed in from off camera, and the band members catch them, turn, and add them to the pyramid. Then two little dogs trot in and start circling around the band's feet. Those dogs scurry off, and three more dogs come in, right on cue with the music. They pose identically with their paws up on three wastebaskets, then

OK Go–
Dogs

run off together. When the guys sit down on four of the wastebaskets, yet another dog comes crashing through the pyramid from behind, runs straight at the camera, and jumps right over it.

What follows is a delightful three minutes of precise dog-human-furniture choreography with the white-clad band members, white Ikea tables, chairs, shelves, and wastebaskets, and 12 adorable, mismatched mongrels. The video ends with the dogs, the furniture, and the band members all forming a three-level pyramid (or "dogamid," as Sie calls it) and crisply bowing and raising their heads in (almost) exact time to the music.

Just like *A Million Ways* and *Here It Goes Again* (and *Evolution of Dance* and *The Sneezing Baby Panda* and so many other viral hits),

White Knuckles was shot with a single, fixed camera and was posted to YouTube without edits.

The video went viral almost immediately, amassing a million views in the first 24 hours. Today it has had over 14 million.

Performing with animals is not easy, and working with multiple animals is even harder. Sie and the band certainly could have shot the video using the conventional method for working with animals in film and television: shooting in short takes, capturing one stunt, stopping, capturing another, and so on for the entire shoot, and then putting together a heavily edited video that would have simulated an actual start-to-finish performance. But they knew that wasn't what they wanted. They knew they needed to capture everything in one uninterrupted take. So they did the work. It took 124 separate takes until Sie and the band had what they needed. In the end it was Take 72 that was the keeper. According to animal trainer Roland Sonnenburg, of the 124 total takes, there were 10 that were great, but Take 72 had what they wanted: "Somehow it came across on screen that this was real and had integrity," said Sonnenburg. And that was key to helping the video go viral.

Resist Conventional Production Techniques

Whether or not you're working with a dozen dogs, staying away from edits and pans and zooms can be tough. We're all used to thinking that flashier is better and somehow more professional. After all, it's what we see every day on television. Even when you understand that simpler is better, it can be hard to resist the sparkly allure of conventional production techniques, but when you're trying to make viral videos, *keep it simple.*

Like Judson Laipply, OK Go, and other viral video creators who have had such success with this approach, bring that keep-it-simple attitude to every part of your video: costumes, sets, lights, sound, editing, and everything else should all be simple and true. Don't dress it up. Just press record and do it.

And if it turns out that your content isn't strong enough to stand on its own without television-style production tricks, there is a solution: get better content.

We should say that again: if your content isn't strong enough to stand on its own without television style production tricks, *get better content.*

CHAPTER 5

I Am the Camera.
Take Me There.

LIPDUB–I Gotta Feeling (Comm-UQAM 2009)

Because viral video is about giving your audience the unfiltered experience of being right there at your sideshow, recording the action with a single, uninterrupted shot is almost always the best way to go. *David After Dentist, Leave Britney Alone!, The Sneezing Baby Panda*, and *Chocolate Rain* are just a few examples of this. On occasion, however, a single, static camera won't capture the action. In videos like our *Extreme Diet Coke & Mentos Experiments II—The Domino Effect*, where we triggered 250 Coke and Mentos geysers in one big chain reaction, or OK Go's giant Rube Goldberg machine for *This*

Links to These Examples

Too Shall Pass, the action can be so spread out that the camera must move to capture it.

Even so, you still want to show us something real, and you want nothing to interfere with that truth. When you have to move the camera, you can use this simple idea to shape how you do it: *I am the camera; take me there.*

To foster the direct, personal connection you have with your audience in online video, treat the camera as if it were a real person watching the action with you.

Film and television directors move their cameras all over the set, but with viral video, the camera is the viewer. Ideally, don't move it at all. Nor should you put it in places where a real person wouldn't be. Don't have it float through the scene on a crane or on a dolly because a real person watching the action as it unfolds wouldn't be able to do that. When you use those kinds of camera moves, you're telling your audience, "This isn't real."

With this metaphor, a sudden close-up can be like yanking us off our feet and dragging us toward the subject. Switching to another camera is like teleporting us across the room or up onto the roof.

Edits to new camera angles raise questions of honesty: Is this really what happened, or did you do everything all over again for a second camera? The less you mess with us and the fewer questions we ask about how you captured this on video, the better.

Just take us there.

The easiest way to do this is what we saw in the last chapter: just press record and do it. That's the cleanest way to keep it real.

But when absolutely necessary, there are a few specific kinds of edits and camera moves that can work, and they all follow the mantra: I am the camera; take me there.

You still want to simply press record and say "Action." And when you say "Cut," your video should be as close to ready for the Internet as possible.

Move the Camera as If It Is a Person

When the action is too big to fit in one frame and you have to move the camera, move it as if it were a person walking exactly where a real person would walk. Again, show us what it would truly be like if we were there.

Another OK Go video is a nice example of this. When the band wanted to shoot a giant Rube Goldberg machine synchronized with their song "This Too Shall Pass," a single, fixed camera just couldn't capture it.

OK Go—Rube
Goldberg

The huge chain reaction, designed by the LA-based Syyn Labs, used over 700 household items along a half-mile-long course. As with *White Knuckles* with all those dogs, conventional television producers would have shot the video in pieces, with multiple cameras capturing the action in many different takes from many different angles. They would have put it all together later, in the editing room.

But OK Go stayed true.

They used a single Steadicam (a smooth, stabilized handheld camera). It moved along the course of the chain reaction to create a video that makes us feel like we are right there. It followed exactly the path we would have chosen to walk along to see the events unfold and at such a pace that we could have kept up.

It took two days of filming and about 60 takes to get it right. And we are the camera, witnessing this extraordinary feat. That's contagious. And it has had 36 million views.

Similarly, the entire genre of lip dub videos often requires a moving camera. A *lip dub* is a single-shot video of a group of people lip-synching to a song, with the original audio of the song dubbed on top. With the people spread throughout a building or even throughout an entire town, the camera moves from person to person, as each one in turn picks up the lip-synch. One of the best examples of the genre is *LIPDUB—I Gotta Feeling (Comm-UQAM 2009)* (10 million views).

Directed by Luc-Olivier Cloutier and Marie-Ève Hébert, two students at the Université du Québec à Montréal (UQAM), the video takes us through one of the campus's central buildings as 172 students—with costumes, props, and choreography lip synch the Black Eyed Peas' hit "I Gotta Feeling."

LIPDUB–
I Gotta
Feeling

After extensive preparation by the organizers, they were able to get what they wanted with just two rehearsals and two takes. It was an extraordinary undertaking, and much of the video's power comes from the truth. Watching the video, you *know* the organizers had to pull off this elaborate stunt in a single shot.

As OK Go did with their Rube Goldberg machine, Cloutier and Hébert's *LIPDUB* showed us something real. They just pressed record, and they took us there. The truth of the event was supported beautifully by the way they filmed it.

So only move the camera when it is absolutely necessary, and when you must move it, remember: I am the camera.

Edit Only to Take Out the Boring Parts

Just as you must resist the temptation to move the camera, you must resist the temptation to cut from one shot to another. Any edit that changes perspective triggers our orienting response and interferes with our unfiltered experience of being there with you.

The only tolerable edits in viral video are ones that honestly move us forward in time.

Scotsman Danny MacAskill's stunt bicycle videos for Red Bull and Inspired Bicycles, *Way Back Home* (21 million views) and *Inspired Bicycles* (31 million views), both show sequences of amazing bike tricks, one after another after another. In *Inspired Bicycles*, MacAskill even attempts to ride along the top of a wrought iron fence that is nothing more than a long row of spikes. After a couple of impressive but unsuccessful tries, he finally nails it, riding all the way across the entire 18- to 20-foot section. From there, the video goes into a mind-boggling series of stunt riding tricks performed in locations all over Edinburgh.

Inspired Bicycles

It's not all done in one shot. MacAskill doesn't waste our time by showing us all the times he had to get himself up and dust himself off to try again. He doesn't drag things out with shots of him riding from one stunt location to the next. In this case, one uninterrupted shot would make it a long, boring video. So he gives us just the highlights, in many pieces. But within each piece, the video follows the rules. Each individual stunt is shot with a single camera and with as little camera movement as possible. The edits he makes don't change our perspective; they just move us forward in time. They only cut out the boring parts without interfering with the truth. Most important, they don't filter our experience of the stunt and make us subconsciously question whether what we're seeing is real.

Editing *Diet Coke & Mentos*

The core of our first Coke and Mentos video was shot in one take with a single camera out in a friend's field. In fact, what you see on the video was, at that point, the first and only time we'd ever set off so many geysers.

When we looked at the footage, there were two problems: first, we realized that for the audience to understand what we were doing, we needed to make clear that we were simply dropping Mentos candies into bottles of Coke; and second, one pair of geysers didn't go off,

The Extreme Diet Coke & Mentos Experiments

and we didn't have the opportunity to go back and try again to get it all perfect in one take.

To address the first problem, we added a couple of short additional shots at the beginning to show how the basic Coke and Mentos geyser works. To address the second problem, we edited out the two geysers that didn't work. If you watch the video closely, you might notice one cut in the core of the video where we removed the footage of the two duds.

If we could have, we would've gone back and done it all in one take. We just didn't have it in us to set up another 101 bottles. As it stands, we can live with the edits because, like Danny MacAskill's bicycle videos, each part of the video follows the rules.

The edits are not the edits of television, where moving the viewpoint is used relentlessly to keep the viewer's attention. In our video, the content keeps the viewer's attention. The edits merely pick up the action a few seconds or a few minutes down the road. They stay true to: I am the camera; take me there. With this style of limited editing, we can still feel as though we're right there, live, at your sideshow.

Edits that stay true by removing only the boring parts are particularly useful for video blogs and online series like *My Drunk Kitchen* where the blogger can ramble on and on in front of a fixed camera and then use edits to move us from one good part to the next. The viral web series *Ask a Ninja* pioneered the use of this technique to record, then edit down improvisational comedy rants, making each episode, in essence, a highlight reel. The edits condense a long improv session into a great few minutes with tight comedic timing.

My Drunk Kitchen   Ask a Ninja

Here's the test: does your edit honestly carry us forward in time, or does it just change our perspective on the action? If it honestly carries us forward in time, it's probably still true. If it just changes our perspective, it's probably not.

⏵ *Some Videos Like the UQAM Lipdub Are Clearly Staged. Does This Make Them Not True?*

Being true doesn't mean being unplanned.

Some viral videos capture reality as it happens. A little kid biting his brother's finger in *Charlie Bit My Finger—Again* or the epic battle between lions, crocodiles, and water buffalo in *Battle at Kruger* show us amazing spontaneous events.

But like some of the elaborately staged (but real) marriage proposals we have mentioned and like OK Go's Rube Goldberg machine and UQAM's lip dub, many contagious videos are very carefully planned reality. They do more than just happening to stumble across real situations and less than just faking them. They create intriguing moments by staging interesting, real situations and then capturing what really happens when real people encounter them. The sword swallower, the fire eater, and the snake charmer at the sideshow are all real, but they also give well-planned performances.

So you can plan, even practice, for an event you're going to shoot for your video, as we do for all our videos. You can set up 100 bottles of Diet Coke in the woods and choreograph and rehearse a two-minute Coke and Mentos geyser show. Just don't fake it with hidden garden hoses or show staged audience reaction shots—stay true.

Evolution of Dance is literally staged—on an actual stage—and it's an honest documentation of a performance that really happened. It is an extremely well-rehearsed dance, and the video simply captures that dance in front of a live audience. There's nothing fake about that. The real, live energy has a contagiousness that *Disneyland Musical Marriage Proposal*, which is false from the beginning, can never have.

So while it's a good idea to get rid of the actors and throw away the script, you don't have to go in without a plan in order to show us something true.

CHAPTER 6

FOR MARKETERS:
Be Honest

Coca-Cola Happiness Machine

We shouldn't have to say this, but we do. Be honest.

You're developing a cool new video for your brand, one that shows how your brand is hip and how well you relate to your customers. Wouldn't it be great if someone else "spontaneously" uploaded it to YouTube without you? Better yet, they could upload it to a video contest you're sponsoring and announce: look at what we just posted without the company's knowledge! That would further all your goals but have no appearance of brand involvement. That would look unplanned and authentic.

We were once asked to do exactly that. We declined.

We have always tried to be honest in acknowledging our sponsors. They make our videos possible, and that's great for everyone. There is every reason to embrace that.

And we've always tried to be clear that we don't work from scripts that ensure that all the brand messages are delivered as they would be in a television commercial. We create true events and capture honest reactions. Your brand can do that too. In the world of viral video, it's a stronger choice.

A lot of brands want to "improve" on reality by scripting everything, using actors, and trying to conceal their involvement, as we saw with *Disneyland Musical Marriage Proposal*. Resist these temptations. Just be honest.

To see what it's like when you keep it honest and do it for real, let's look at *Coca-Cola Happiness Machine* (4.8 million views).

Nothing Was Scripted

Coca-Cola Happiness Machine begins with a janitor loading a vending machine in a college campus lounge. Then the machine starts

Coca-Cola
Happiness
Machine

dispensing some surprising items. First, instead of a single bottle of soda, one student gets bottle after bottle after bottle. For another student, a hand reaches out from the machine with a bouquet of flowers. Eventually even a pizza and an enormous sandwich pop out.

And Coca-Cola made it honestly.

They created the circumstances, *Candid Camera* style, but from there on, everything was authentic. There were no actors, and there was no set. We see real people through real hidden cameras, and Coca-Cola was careful not to do anything to undermine that. Everything rings true.

As AJ Brustein, global senior brand manager for Coca-Cola, explained to *Mashable*:

> Coke's goal was to create an organic experience. Other than the janitor loading the machine, nothing was scripted. If the video had been scripted, it wouldn't have had the same effect. The girl

mouthing "Oh My God," students helping each other lift the
huge sub, hugging the Coke machine—these true moments are
what gave the video life.

So *Coca-Cola Happiness Machine* or *Disneyland Musical Marriage Proposal*? Which do you want to pass along to your friends? Which creates positive emotion, the truth or the lie? Which will build a strong, ongoing relationship with your viewers, the truth or the lie?

With the *Happiness Machine*, there was no need to be reticent about acknowledging Coca-Cola's involvement. Nor was there any need to script the piece with all the precise brand messaging of a television spot. Coke found something even better—and more viral—by keeping it true.

Be honest. Guard your authenticity every step of the way. It's important currency in the world of viral video.

Trying to Keep a Secret

A cautionary tale of a company trying and failing to pull the wool over everyone's eyes comes from the blogging world. Its lessons apply just as strongly to sponsoring viral videos. Please don't do what Walmart did back in 2006 (back when they were Wal-Mart, with a hyphen).

In September of that year, a couple named Jim and Laura started a blog called *Wal-Marting Across America*. They posted stories and photos of their trip across the country, parking their RV in Walmarts along the way. They blogged about Walmart's environmental efforts, about how Walmart employees benefited from their health insurance, and more.

Soon, however, people started asking who was footing the bill.

In less than two weeks, it was all over.

Jim and Laura were revealed to be a photographer at the *Washington Post* and a freelance writer. They really had had the idea to take a trip and spend their nights in Walmart parking lots, but

"Working Families for Wal-Mart," an organization started by Wal-mart's PR firm Edelman and funded by Walmart, took the idea, expanded it, organized it, and paid for it.

What was initially going to be a short trip to visit their children became a cross-country odyssey in an RV with a Working Families for Wal-Mart logo on it.

After *Businessweek.com* uncovered the truth, *Wal-Marting Across America* went on to make *CNN Money*'s list of the year's 101 Dumbest Moments in Business. *CNN Money* wrote:

> The stunt is especially bad news for Edelman, since it violates ethical guidelines it helped to write for the nascent Word of Mouth Marketing Association.

You would think they would have known better, particularly since this wasn't their first problem with the blogosphere. Four months before *Wal-Marting Across America*, Walmart and Edelman were caught feeding pro-Walmart stories to bloggers. Alyce Lomax of the *Motley Fool* wrote at the time:

> Wal-Mart's strategy to repair its public image through the blogosphere has resoundingly backfired. News like this makes the company sound sneaky and underhanded, out to launch the equivalent of a corporate propaganda campaign, which of course fires up Wal-Mart's detractors even more.

They got caught and caught again. Not the image rehabilitation that Walmart would have liked. Not the reputation you want. Not the relationship you want to build with your customers.

Mind you, no one knows what deceptive campaigns have worked and haven't been uncovered, but it's hard to keep a secret these days.

In a 2011 *New York Times* article, "Upending Anonymity: These Days the Web Unmasks Everyone," Brian Stelter pointed out:

The collective intelligence of the Internet's two billion users, and the digital fingerprints that so many users leave on Web sites, combine to make it more and more likely that every embarrassing video, every intimate photo, and every indelicate e-mail is attributed to its source, whether that source wants it to be or not.

During the riots in Vancouver after the 2011 Stanley Cup finals, an unidentified couple was photographed lying on the ground kissing amid the chaos. The photo spread like wildfire, along with the question, "Who are these people?" In a matter of *hours*, the collective efforts of people on the Internet had pieced things together and had identified the couple. How long would it take those 2 billion users to root out who was behind a faked blog or who sponsored a bogus viral video?

Tell the Simple Truth

Why try to pull the wool over our eyes? Whatever pressure you face, don't try to conceal things. Be honest.

You can be involved. You can sponsor videos. Just be up front about it. Be like Office Max, ABC Family, and our other sponsors, and be straightforward in embracing your involvement. Be like Stride Gum with the *Where the Hell Is Matt?* videos, with a simple and strong closing title card on the video: "Thanks to Stride for making this possible."

Like Coca-Cola did with its *Happiness Machine* success, don't worry about getting every brand message perfectly delivered. Keep it real, and find something even better. As John Grant has written in his book *The New Marketing Manifesto*, "Authenticity is the benchmark against which all brands are now judged."

You can use online video to build a strong, honest, authentic relationship with your consumers. That positive emotion isn't just good for your brand. It'll also help you go viral.

Don't Waste My Time

Less chitchat, more swallowing.

—Natasha Veruschka, The Queen of Swords

Most attempts at viral video take too long to get down to business.

On the Internet, your audience can leave whenever they want. And they will. If they get bored, they'll be gone in an instant.

We all know that feeling, when we're watching the first few seconds of a video, on the fence, judging, waiting to see whether or not it will be worth it. Sometimes before we even consciously realize it, our hands are reaching to click to something else.

Getting down to business can be the difference between a few thousand views and a few million views. To see this, we looked at videos of breakdance battles on YouTube. There are a few great videos, like *Breakdance Hip Hop Battle* and *Battle of the Year 2010,* each with millions of views. But when you get past the top few, you find videos like *One on One Breakdance Battle—Red Bull BC One Cypher 2012 Bulgaria* that has had only 35,000 views. What's the difference?

One on One is a slickly produced video. It begins with a guy with spiky hair walking through an ancient amphitheater talking about the great breakdancing battle that's going to happen later on at a club. Then there are beautiful shots of a cityscape, of spectators watching dancers, of people taking classes, of a few Red Bull cans and logos, of more talking about breakdancing.... In the first *30 seconds*, there's only *one* interesting dance move. The first time we get to see clips of the dance contest is at 1:41 into the video, and it doesn't really kick into gear until we're a full two minutes in. Shots of dancers are then intercut with shots of the crowd, the sound mixing board, the judges, and more people talking about breakdancing, sometimes while holding a can of Red Bull. Altogether, it's five minutes long, and it's had 35,000 views.

One on One Breakdance Battle–Red Bull BC One Cypher 2012 Bulgaria

Breakdance Hip Hop Battle, on the other hand, is shot with a single camera in a large room with bad fluorescent lighting. Music is playing, and a young man steps into the center, and within five seconds, he's dancing. Within fourteen seconds, the crowd around the edge of the room is hooting and hollering encouragement. For the next six minutes, the dancers trade off and show us what they've got, one move after another. Nothing else. It's had 9.6 million views.

Breakdance Hip Hop Battle

With *One on One*, warning bells were already going off with all those edits, camera angles, and other disruptive production techniques. But most of all, the video just takes too long to deliver. We want to watch people breakdancing, so showing us people talking is wasting our time. It turns out that once *One on One* gets going, the dancing is spectacular, but online if you're going to make us wait two minutes for the good stuff, we're leaving.

Online video is sideshow, vaudeville, street performing. And the street corner is one of the harshest performing venues ever invented. On the street, the audience is always one step from walking away. If you've ever been one of those audience members, you know that feeling: you just want to keep walking by; you don't want to stop. A street performer has to get people to stop. He has to get those people to stay and watch while he gets more people to stop. Then he has to keep all of those people entertained while building that small group into a bigger crowd. And then once he's got a good crowd, he has to keep them all from getting bored and leaving so that they're there at the end when he passes the hat. If street performing teaches you anything, it teaches you to *always be interesting.* If you break that rule for even as little as a minute, your audience will start to disappear, your tips will be meager, and you might not have money for your dinner that night.

Online, it's the same. You need to think like a street performer: people out there are busy doing other things, so you need to grab them, keep them watching, and refuse to give them a chance to walk away.

So show us what you've got, and don't waste our time for even a moment. If we're here to see the sword swallower, show us the sword swallower. Right away. Maybe the best at this is *Dramatic Chipmunk* (actually a prairie dog, that turns suddenly to the camera with striking theatrical flair). It delivers its sideshow moment right away, and then it's done. It's five seconds long. And 36 million people have watched.

Dramatic Chipmunk

Get down to business and then don't overstay your welcome. *Charlie Schmidt's Keyboard Cat!—THE ORIGINAL!* (25 million views) and *Skateboarding Dog* (20 million views) both deliver on the promises of their titles within three seconds. Neither of those videos, however, can hold its audience for very long. After perhaps a minute, we get it and we're ready to move on.

So whether your video will be five seconds long, five minutes long, or longer,

Keyboard Cat   Skateboard-ing Dog

be ruthless. Make sure there isn't a second more than is absolutely necessary.

To succeed online, you need to put your video through a brutal editing process: How badly do you need those two seconds? You probably don't. Is that reverse angle shot necessary? It probably isn't. Show us what you've got, and then wrap it up. Don't waste our time.

An Agonizing 58 Seconds

Despite our best efforts, our third viral hit, *The Extreme Sticky Note Experiments*, didn't get right down to business, and it suffered for it. We made that video in Los Angeles in partnership with Disney and ABC Family, and we were working with a talented team of Hollywood directors, actors, and producers. Although the piece got millions of views online and won some great industry awards, it wasn't what it could have been.

The Extreme Sticky Note Experiments

The piece uses over 250,000 sticky notes, transformed into colorful wheels and paper waterfalls, with pads walking down steps like Slinkys and tens of thousands of sticky notes falling from the ceiling.

We tried hard to convince our partners to go with our pure, single-take viral style, but despite our efforts, the heavy influence of traditional TV and movie production sensibilities is evident throughout the video. Most tellingly—and the single biggest reason we think the piece didn't get even more views— is that it takes *an agonizing 58 seconds before we get to the good stuff.* It takes 40 seconds before we even introduce what we're about to do. Before that are shots that establish that we're in an office, shots that establish various characters who are there with us, and so on. The problem was, we had all kinds of fun, crazy creations that we had built using a quarter of a million sticky notes, but we made our audience wait for almost a minute before we showed them any of that.

In Internet video time, that's an eternity, and we know we lost viewers by the hundreds of thousands in that precious first minute. We could see it in the YouTube analytics. If those viewers had stayed for the good stuff, they could have told more people who in turn could have told still more, who in turn..., but it was not to be. Once we lost them, neither they, their friends, nor their friends' friends ever got to see the good stuff.

It may seem hard to argue with the millions of views we got, but we know it could have been so much more. The title promises *The Extreme Sticky Note Experiments.* We needed to show our viewers some sticky notes, and fast.

On TV, having another 58 seconds of well-shot filler is fine. Padding things out with establishing shots and other window dressing is much easier than coming up with another 58 seconds of crazy sticky note stunts. But online, you don't have to fill a timeslot, so just give us the essentials. If what you've got is really just 5 seconds, great. Show us 5 seconds and make them kick ass.

Cutting it down to the bare essentials like this is hard. Even Danny MacAskill's *Inspired Bicycles* struggles a bit with this. That video starts slowly with a series of establishing shots of Edinburgh Castle at sunset over which the words "Inspired presents" appear (0:00 through 0:11). Then we see a series of shots of MacAskill on his bicycle, pedaling casually up a tree-lined path toward the camera over which the words "Danny MacAskill" appear (0:11 through 0:21). Next, a series of shots shows us (1) a close-up of the top of a wrought iron fence, (2) a road sign that says "Tickets and Regulations," (3) MacAskill pedaling his bicycle, and (4) MacAskill removing the "Tickets and Regulations" sign from the sidewalk and walking out of frame with it (0:21 through 0:33).

Inspired
Bicycles

It's not until 35 seconds into the video that we finally get to see MacAskill ride his bike up to a large city utility box and astonish us by jumping almost straight up the five feet or so required to land balanced on top of it.

Nice trick. But it was an awfully long time getting there.

At that point the video takes off and the unforgettable content that earned it 29 million views kicks in. It moves seamlessly from one amazing trick to the next at a wonderfully relaxed, yet riveting pace so that it's almost impossible *not* to watch from there all the way to the end. Even this fantastic video, though, could have held more viewers and been even more contagious if it had gotten down to business faster. How many views would *Inspired Bicycles* have had if the producers had simply cut the first 30 seconds of the video?

Try watching it yourself, starting at 0:30 and see what you think. Try watching our sticky note video starting at 0:40. For our money, they're both stronger and more contagious without the preliminary establishing shots.

In the first few seconds of your video, you have to convince people that they should keep watching. Then you have to keep convincing them, moment by moment, to stick with you all the way through until you're done. So as soon as the viewer clicks "play," start delivering.

CHAPTER 7

Nothing but the Money Shots

The Extreme Diet Coke & Mentos Experiments

Whenever possible, make your video nothing but money shots. If you're promising us extreme sticky note experiments, show us extreme sticky note experiments. Nothing else. If you're promising us a guy wiping out on a skateboard or a cute puppy falling asleep, show us a guy wiping out on a skateboard or a cute puppy falling asleep. Immediately.

What's a money shot?

In movies, money shots are the provocative, sensational, or spectacular sequences that make a film memorable. They're what the audience has paid to see. Done well, they can be what makes a film unforgettable. They're Thelma and Louise driving their car as fast as they can over the edge of the Grand Canyon and plummeting to their death, the classic slow motion bullet-time sequence from *The Matrix*, and the indelibly gross chestburster scene in *Alien*. In TV news, they're the footage of the tornado, the tsunami, or the building collapsing. In newspapers and magazines, they're the shot of the car going off the bridge or the house that was flattened by the gas explosion. They're the moments that people talk about when they're leaving the theater and when they're around the water cooler the next day.

In viral video, you want every moment to be a money shot. That's how to hold your audience online. Think of it as performing on the street corner, where every audience member is constantly one step away from walking away. Don't give them an opportunity to leave. Keep people from clicking away from your video by giving them just the good stuff—nothing but the money shots.

When we refer to *money shots* for viral video, we're talking about a little more than just the explosions. Not a lot more, but a little. In viral video, we think of the money shots as anything that gives us the information we want when we want it. To see what that means, and what shots are absolutely necessary, it helps to look at the structure of sideshow acts.

Setup and Payoff

The structure of sideshow is setup and payoff. The payoff is the main event: the sword swallower. The setup is what we need to know—and only what we need to know—to understand what we're about to see. For example, is it a real sword?

In your viral video, ask yourself: what is absolutely *essential* for us to understand before we see the explosions? It may be absolutely nothing. That's great. We don't need any setup to understand a dog riding a skateboard. Just show us your skateboarding dog. For other videos, some setup may be needed. You can't tell us just the punch line to a joke without the setup. We won't get it. The same is true for viral video. If a setup shot provides crucial information, keep it. *If not, get rid of it.*

Each of our videos follows this setup and payoff structure, and we aim for nothing but the money shots.

For example, our first Coke and Mentos video promises 101 bottles of Coke shooting 20 feet into the air. It took some work to figure out what shots were necessary.

The Extreme Diet Coke & Mentos Experiments

When we first showed the rough footage to our friends, we showed them just the 101-bottle performance (what now begins at 0:28 in the final video). One of those friends, Fritz's former juggling partner (and since then, longtime Cirque du Soleil performer) Steve Ragatz, gave us the blunt, yet invaluable note: "Great—but frankly I can't quite understand what's going on."

Watching the footage again with Steve's note in mind, we realized that the 101-bottle performance alone—what we thought were the money shots—didn't make clear exactly what we were doing to make all those geysers. As a result, the whole piece was confusing.

To understand the payoff in that video, the audience needed to know two things: (1) we were using nothing but Coke and Mentos—no weird chemicals, no garden hoses, and (2) when you drop a handful of Mentos into a bottle of Coke, the Coke explodes out of the bottle and into the air. Once we made that clear, the audience would understand what was going to happen when they saw the 101 bottles all set up and ready to go.

With that in mind, we then went back and added footage that begins with a shot of the two of us looking soberly straight into the camera: Stephen holding up a two-liter bottle of Diet Coke and Fritz displaying a single roll of Mentos, followed by a title card saying "Experiment #4," followed by a second title card saying "2 liters of Diet Coke/4 Mentos." We included those to make clear that we were using nothing but soda and candy. That was information the audience needed in order to understand what we were about to do.

We then cut to a simple single-bottle demonstration that showed the 15-foot geyser you can get when you drop a handful of Mentos into a bottle of Diet Coke. That was all the audience needed to know to understand the payoff: 101 bottles of Coke and 523 Mentos.

So to enjoy *The Extreme Diet Coke & Mentos Experiments*, do you need to know who we are? Where we are? Do you need to know that we spent six months developing this stunt? You do need to understand what the heck we're doing.

Just show me the money. Show me 101 bottles of Coke spraying into the air and the essential setup to understand that payoff.

Minimum Setup, Maximum Payoff

What's the lesson? Get down to business as fast as possible, but don't rush into your payoff until you're sure your audience will understand it. Once they do, get down to it. For *The Extreme Diet Coke & Mentos Experiments*, that meant adding those first explanatory 30 seconds and then going right into the payoff. On the other hand, for *Evolution of Dance*, the setup is nothing more than the announcer's voice over the PA system saying "Evolution. Of dance." Then the payoff begins. Videos that go viral, videos like *JK Wedding Entrance Dance*, OK Go's videos, and *Keyboard Cat*, don't waste our time. They give us nothing but the money shots.

In putting together your own viral videos, you'll have to find the balance between setup and payoff that works for you, but remember, as soon as the viewer clicks "play," get down to business. Include enough information so that you're sure your viewers will understand what's going on. But once you do, show us what you've got. Show us your bike tricks. Set off your 101 geysers. Start dancing. Don't wait a second longer than you have to to show us what you've got that's unforgettable.

⏵ *How Long Should a Viral Video Be?*

Thirty seconds? Two to three minutes? Ten minutes? The conventional wisdom is that a viral video should be no longer than two to three minutes, but we haven't seen good evidence to support this.

Our answer is this: a viral video should be only as long as it needs to be for the audience to appreciate and understand the money shots, but no longer. Our *Experiment #137* (2:57) and *Experiment #214* (3:02) were both about three minutes, but *The Sneezing Baby Panda* (140 million views) is only seventeen seconds long, and *Battle at Kruger* (67 million views) is over eight full minutes. What's similar about all of these isn't their length, but rather that each of them is nothing but money shots—then they're over. That's how you want *your* video to be.

The
Sneezing
Baby
Panda

Battle at
Kruger

There is no set length for what works online. *The Sneezing Baby Panda* wouldn't have worked at *Battle at Kruger*'s eight minutes, and *Battle at Kruger* wouldn't have worked chopped down to seventeen seconds.

Look at *The Sneezing Baby Panda*. That viral video classic is nothing more than a fixed camera shot of a panda in a cage chewing contentedly on bamboo with its cub sleeping peacefully at its feet. When the cub sneezes suddenly and startles the adult panda, for some reason that moment is pretty darn funny, perhaps because we can all imagine ourselves there, having that same reaction. The setup here includes an important, short interlude of quiet—just a few seconds of chewing—that builds our anticipation and keeps us guessing when the moment of action will happen. Then, once we've seen the startling sneeze and the reaction, we're done, so the video should be over. In *The Sneezing Baby Panda*, seventeen seconds for this setup and payoff is just about perfect.

At the other end of the spectrum, *Battle at Kruger* is nothing but money shots for over eight minutes. Almost all of those eight minutes are a single uninterrupted, handheld shot filmed during a safari in South Africa's Kruger National Park. The video begins looking across a watering hole at a herd of buffalo. The camera pans right to show a pride of lions, crouched down in the grass, stalking the buffalo. The tension builds until finally the lions charge, scatter the buffalo, and manage to separate a calf from the herd. But their attack knocks the calf into the water, and as the lions wade in to grab the calf to pull it out, a crocodile rises out of the water and seizes the calf in its jaws. It's now a deadly game of tug-of-war between the lions and the crocodile.

The lions slowly pull the hapless calf away from the crocodile and up onto dry land. Then, just as the crocodile swims away and the lions settle in for the kill, the entire herd of buffalo *returns*, charges the lions, chases them off, and saves their calf. Miraculously, the calf is able to walk off, with no apparent injuries, to rejoin the herd.

Every second of this video is riveting. Even the first minute before the confrontation is compelling because we see the buffalo unwittingly heading directly toward the pride of lions to what we know might mean death for at least one of them. And when the confrontation is over and the calf is safe, the video is over. From start to finish it's nothing but money shots.

Seventeen seconds of *The Sneezing Panda*. Eight minutes of *Battle at Kruger*. Both nothing but the money shots. Which is exactly what you want *your* videos to be.

If you work really hard to keep your audience there, moment by moment, videos even longer than *Battle at Kruger* can still be successful.

Star Wars: The Phantom Menace Review

Star Wars: The Phantom Menace Review, a brilliant, detailed, and often-hilarious home-made review of one of the weakest episodes in the *Star Wars* franchise, is *seventy minutes* long, and it has had 1.2 million views (and three times that for the first ten-minute segment). Holding an audience for that long online is an amazing achievement, but as *The Phantom Menace Review* shows, it can be done.

CHAPTER 8

Don't Tell Me a Story

Evolution of Dance

This may sound sacrilegious, but the evidence for it is overwhelming. Contrary to popular belief, and unlike all other film and video, viral video is not about story.

Viral video is the twenty-first-century sideshow, and the sideshow isn't about story. It's all about the hook and delivering on the hook.

This means don't waste our time with irrelevant narrative. What is irrelevant narrative?

Just about all of it.

Do we want to know the sword swallower's life story? No. We want to see him swallow swords.

Do we care why the *Will It Blend?* guy wants to blend an iPhone? No. We want to see it gloriously destroyed.

The Power of Stories

We don't want to dismiss the power of stories. Humans are drawn to stories. Television, film, advertising, and sales—all of these use storytelling to great effect. Randall Rothenberg and Mike Hughes have pointed out in *AdAge Blogs*, "In advertising specifically, the art and craft of storytelling is central to building, maintaining and strengthening the bonds between consumers and brands."

In their book *Made to Stick*, Chip Heath and Dan Heath argue: "How do we get people to act on our ideas? We tell stories."

But viral video is different. For viral video, the idea of storytelling is an obstacle.

If you promise us a baby monkey riding backward on a pig, anything that gets in the way of seeing a baby monkey riding backward on a pig is wasting our time. As *Time* magazine's *NewsFeed* put it: "Baby Monkey Riding a Baby Pig—Enough Said."

Baby Monkey (Going Backwards on a Pig)

It's no accident that almost none of the top videos of all time on YouTube is there to tell a story. The list includes music videos, novelty songs, a laughing baby, a crazy dance, a kid biting his brother's finger, a sneezing panda, and on and on. These aren't stories. They're sideshows. True, occasionally something like a Lady Gaga music video includes a bit of a story, but no one watches Lady Gaga for the story. They watch for the great, over-the-top sideshow performances she puts on.

In fact, the top videos on YouTube are almost all classic vaudeville, classic sideshow.

Links to These Examples

From the earliest days of online video, it's been that way. There are no stories being told in *Dancing Baby* (1996), *Dancing Banana/It's Peanut Butter Jelly Time* (2001), *Star Wars Kid* (2002), or *Numa Numa* (2004). Like almost all other viral hits, those videos are about what's crazy, weird, or funny—indeed, everything *but* story.

The lack of story online has continued in *Evolution of Dance, David After Dentist, Chocolate Rain, Leave Britney Alone!, The Extreme Diet Coke & Mentos Experiments, JK Wedding Entrance Dance,* OK Go's many viral hits, *Improv Everywhere,* and beyond.

There's still a powerful temptation to try to tell a story in online video, but thinking of viral video as traditional narrative pulls you in directions that get away from what will make your video go viral.

We don't have time for the hero's journey. Give us sideshow.

Death by Story

Let's look again for a moment at our video *The Extreme Sticky Note Experiments.* As we've noted, in that video we took almost a minute before we got to anything people might want to share online.

What happened? Narrative happened. This is one of the clearest examples of narrative getting in the way.

Because that video was to debut simultaneously online and on television, there was pressure from the sponsors to frame it more for television.

The Extreme Sticky Note Experiments

To them, that meant narrative.

So instead of getting down to business and showing the crazy things we'd created with sticky notes, the first part of that video was a story. We became two mischievous office workers. There was a mean boss. There was an overworked secretary. Early in the video, the mean boss came out of his office and dropped a pile of papers on the desk of the secretary and walked out. But once the boss was gone, the workers could have some fun—here come the sticky note tricks! Then at the end, when the boss returned, the sticky notes were everywhere, and we were in trouble! But then he picked up a pad of sticky notes and started playing with it. Maybe, just maybe, we were starting to change him.

That's what we mean by narrative.

None of that was necessary to appreciate the cool tricks we were about to do with a quarter of a million sticky notes. All you needed to understand was that we were using nothing but sticky notes. After that, it was time to get down to business. We had some amazing visuals, and that's what our audience was there to see—not a story about an overworked secretary and a mean boss. And unfortunately, for that first section of the video, during all that storytelling, the online audience was leaving in droves.

Focus on the Setup and Payoff

The Extreme Sticky Note Experiments still managed to get millions of views, but it had to overcome all that narrative. If we had stuck to the structure of sideshow—minimum setup, maximum payoff—we would have been much better off.

Do you have a cool trick to show us? Great. Show us your trick. Don't tell us your story.

Does your baby start laughing every time you tear a piece of paper? Show us. Don't tell us the story of how you discovered this. Make videos like *The Sneezing Panda, Battle at Kruger, Numa Numa,* and all the other top videos on YouTube. Forget about story. Focus on sideshow.

Emotion Without Story

Be careful not to confuse lack of narrative with lack of emotion.

One of the places in that sticky note video that people go back to and watch again is near the end when we raise our arms in triumph. That same celebratory gesture is often people's favorite part of our Coke and Mentos videos as well. That moment of triumph is the most fun, emotional part of the video. The emotion in that video doesn't come from the story. It comes from our celebration of what we've just done and the mess we've made with sticky notes.

Emotional videos don't need narrative. There are gut-wrenching examples of this in several compilation videos of soldiers coming home from duty: *Soldier Homecoming Surprise Mix* (9.8 million views), *The Best Surprise Military Homecomings: Part One* (6.3 million views), and others.

Links to These Examples

Reality TV, with a 30- or 60-minute timeslot to fill, would use the narrative approach for this: We'd see the soldier leaving his unit and boarding a plane. We'd see the plane land in Wisconsin and a car take him to his daughter's school. We'd see him walk down the hallway to her classroom.

Online, we don't need that story. Story just wastes our time. We want to see the reunion. All we need to know to understand the payoff is that this soldier is coming home to surprise his daughter, son, or wife. The title of the video alone (*Soldier Homecoming Surprise Mix*) is enough to make that clear. So show us what we're here for: heartbreakingly beautiful reunions. The money shots.

These homecoming videos are some of the most overwhelmingly emotional viral videos online, but even they don't tell a story. They just give us one emotional moment after another.

It Looks Like a Story, but...

Occasionally a video will go viral that looks like a story. Almost always, however, it's still about the sideshow.

In the video *Christian the Lion*, for example (there are many versions online, but the most popular has had 18 million views), we see the story of a lion who was bought as a pet in 1969 and, when he had gotten too big to handle, was released back into the wild. About a year later, his former owners went to Africa to find him, expecting not to be recognized. But Christian did indeed know them, and the video shows him, fully grown and in the wild, leaping up playfully to put his paws on their shoulders and nuzzle their faces.

Christian the Lion

There was a 1971 documentary that told the story of Christian and his former owners.

It was 89 minutes long. The documentary didn't go viral. What went viral was the sideshow moments. The setup and payoff.

The most viewed version of *Christian the Lion* is just 1 minute and 17 seconds in which the only parts of the "story" remaining are those that are essential to understanding the payoff. As with our Coke and Mentos videos, there must be just enough explanation so that you can make sense of what you're about to see. And nothing more.

In *Christian the Lion*, the payoff is seeing a lion out in the wild jump on two guys and *not* kill them. More than telling the story of Christian the lion, the video provides the minimum explanation needed to understand why the lion doesn't rip them to pieces.

It's still classic sideshow. It's setup and payoff. It's the lion tamer.

For the most popular version of this video, the entire story is told in five title cards. That's the setup. And then it gets right to the payoff. No time wasted.

The version that really went viral kept just the sideshow moments and removed the narrative. Unlike the documentary, the viral video didn't have establishing shots showing Christian's former owners, Ace and John, arriving in Africa. We didn't see Christian roaming across the plains with his new lion friends, Mona and Lisa. There was no shot of George Adamson, the conservationist who had been overseeing Christian's reintroduction into the wild, climbing up the hill to see in which direction the lions might be found that day. All those shots were great for the documentary. What worked online, however, was just over a minute of only the sideshow moments. Only the money shots—almost no story at all.

To succeed online, all 89 minutes of the documentary—all that narrative—was boiled down to 20 seconds of setup, 50 seconds of payoff, and 7 seconds of closing message.

That's as close as you should come to telling a story in an online video.

⏵ Don't People Share Stories?

Looking around at the top viral videos, we just don't see it.

Looking through Webby Award winners at what is recognized as some of the best online storytelling produces a list with disappointing view counts. Webby Award winners *Web Therapy* with Lisa Kudrow and *The Office—The Accountants* are beautiful examples of the best of the best, and while they also get views on their own sites, these videos only get in the range of 15,000 to 90,000 views on You-Tube. Unimpressive results for narrative.

Links to These Examples

There are a very few exceptions where videos with stories have had remarkable strengths and have broken through to go viral.

The Landlord, Will Ferrell's groundbreaking video from 2007, was a huge success. It features Pearl, his nasty, swearing, threatening landlord, as played by a cute toddler. There's a certain sideshow element of a tiny toddler in an adorable little dress saying, "Bitch! Bitch! Bitch!" And the then-radical idea of a star like Will Ferrell making an online video made it quite a novelty. It feels like watching his home movies, and it is literally something he and his friends made for fun.

The Landlord

The structure of *The Landlord* is efficient—and it is narrative. It stands with a handful of *Saturday Night Live* sketches, like Tina Fey's uncanny Sarah Palin impersonations, as the rare comedy sketches that have had enough bang to really catch on online.

During the Hollywood writers' strike of 2007–2008, Joss Whedon, Neil Patrick Harris, and the gang also hit it out of the park with *Dr. Horrible's Sing-Along Blog*. This three-episode, 45-minute musical mixes the structure of a blog with the story of a wannabe supervillain.

Dr. Horrible's Sing-Along Blog

There may be other ways of telling a story online that will get these kinds of results, but they're extremely rare. Right now, our feeling is this: if you have Will Ferrell, Tina Fey, Joss Whedon, or Neil Patrick Harris, please consider making more online narrative. If not, don't risk it.

CHAPTER 9

FOR MARKETERS:
No #&$@ing Product Shots

Guys Backflip into Jeans

The time-honored approach in advertising is that lots is good and more is better. Traditional marketers are getting more and more creative about finding ways to get their brand, their logo, and their message in front of consumers as often as humanly possible. As Louise Story noted in the *New York Times*, subway turnstiles have sported Geico logos, fresh eggs in the carton have been stamped with the names of CBS television shows, Verizon has emblazoned its logo on pizza boxes, and US Airways has found advertisers so eager to get their messages in front of consumers that it has even sold ad space on airsickness bags. According to the market research firm Yankelovich, Inc., in the 1980s typical city dwellers had some 2,000 brand messages foisted upon them every day. Today that number is up to 5,000. Per day. Every day.

But conventional branding with its ever-present logos, product shots, and brand messages will kill your video's chances of going viral.

If you load your video with branding, the risk is that it begins to look like an ad, you lose your emotional connection with the viewers, and you don't go viral. Basically, you can have either a video with 20 perfect product shots that gets 25,000 views or a video with 1 nice product shot that gets 2,500,000 views. You can't usually have both.

Most of the time, a product or logo shot simply gets in the way of the content your audience has come to see. To maximize contagiousness, you need a very light brand touch. Don't let your product shot be a waste of our time. Don't let the presence of your brand kill the contagiousness.

To go viral, you want your video to be nothing but money shots, and 9 times out of 10, a product shot is not a money shot. It's an interruption. You can't promise your viewer something awesome and then interrupt with something else. In short, a brand message inserted when the audience is expecting something else isn't a money shot. It's an annoying non sequitur that hurts both your brand and your chances of going viral. You don't want your video weighed down with interruptions of any sort, and interrupting it *with your brand* isn't just going to hurt your chances of going viral. It's going to make the viewers who do see your piece associate your brand with being annoyed.

For your work to go viral, you need to look for ways to seamlessly merge your brand message to the unique, unforgettable content you're hoping will be contagious.

How can you tell if you've done that? How do you know that you've adequately integrated your brand message into your video? There's a simple test.

The way to tell if your product or logo shot is appropriate for a video you're hoping will go viral is to ask yourself this: Is your product shot something your audience *wants* to see? If not, *get rid of it.*

A product or logo shot—or indeed any shot for that matter— works in viral video only when *it provides information the viewer wants when the viewer wants it.* For example, in the *Will It Blend?* videos, the Blendtec product shots are essential to the content. After we see the blender chew up a bag of marbles, we do indeed want to see what kind of blender it is. At that point, the brand name is information we want. That is exactly what you want to do with your brand.

When it comes to product shots, *integrate or eliminate.*

Strategy 1: Be the Content

Ideally, you want to find a way to integrate your brand into the video in a way that would make sense even if your brand weren't a sponsor. For example, take a look at the brand presence in our Coke and Mentos videos or in Levi's *Guys Backflip into Jeans* video. The brands in those videos are organically integrated into the content, so there's no need to insert irrelevant product shots.

Guys
Backflip
into
Jeans

In *The Extreme Diet Coke & Mentos Experiments,* we needed our audience to understand that those huge 25-foot geysers we were making were created using just Diet Coke and Mentos mint candies, so it made perfect sense to show those two products clearly in the beginning of that video and then just to use them throughout.

In Levi's *Guys Backflip into Jeans* (8 million views), a video that consists of a series of progressively more difficult stunts in which guys jump, and eventually backflip, into a pair of Levi's, the iconic Levi's jeans are essential to the premise, and it only makes sense to show them clearly in each stunt.

The best strategy is to integrate your product or brand message organically into your video the way Blendtec, Coke and Mentos, and Levi's have been integrated. But even when there's no easy way to integrate your brand into the content itself, there's great second strategy.

Strategy 2: Be the Source

When product integration isn't an option, a simple and effective solution is to be the source of the content that makes us smile. Take credit for being the cool people who made this cool video happen. Companies like Cadbury, Sony, and T-Mobile have found great success by simply being associated with viral phenomena. Often, the only hint you have that the video was sponsored at all is a title card or two at the end that connect it with the brand.

T-Mobile used this approach effectively in *The T-Mobile Dance* (35 million views), a video inspired by Improv Everywhere, a performance art group renowned for their flash mob videos in which an assortment of people appears in a public place without any warning, does something unexpected, and then melts away, back into the crowd.

The T-Mobile Dance

The T-Mobile Dance begins with a shot of the usual hustle and bustle in London's Liverpool Street Station at 11 o'clock in the morning. After a few seconds, music starts blasting over the PA: "We-e-e-ll, you make me wanna shout...." Right in the middle of the station, a few people start dancing. After a few seconds, the music changes, and even more dancers join in, and we realize that this is a surprise performance, a flash mob, carefully choreographed with lots of dancers hidden among the crowd.

Soon, the floor of the station is covered with dancers—350 altogether—and for about two and a half minutes, they waltz, disco, pop and lock, do the mashed potato, and more. Interspersed throughout the video are shots of passersby stopping to watch and even joining in. It's great.

At the end, two title cards come up: "Life's for Sharing" and a T-Mobile logo with a website address. Out of 2 minutes and 41 seconds, the only brand presence is in the video's title and in the final 7 seconds.

British chocolatier Cadbury has been a master of this approach ever since its classic *Cadbury Gorilla* video from 2007. That year the company was scrambling to find a way to respond to a public relations disaster. Salmonella contamination had been found in some of its chocolate, and the company had been forced to recall 1 million bars of chocolate. Cadbury had taken a £30 million hit to its sales (about $60 million), and it had suffered serious and potentially long-term damage to its reputation.

Cadbury
Gorilla

Faced with a crucial need to take the public's mind off of the salmonella scare and give the brand other, more positive associations, the company jettisoned its traditional advertising approach and hired Fallon London to refocus its advertising on word-of-mouth and viral marketing. Fallon London and creative director Juan Cabral came up with the idea for what became known as the *Cadbury Gorilla* (6.7 million views), a quirky, somewhat puzzling 90-second video in which what appears to be either a gorilla or a person in a convincingly realistic gorilla suit sits at a drum set, drumsticks in hand, listening to Phil Collins's "In the Air Tonight." When the music reaches the drum solo, the gorilla takes over and drums like a rock star. Finally, in the last 5 seconds, the image of the drumming gorilla fades into an image of a Cadbury Dairy Milk chocolate bar and the words "a glass and a half full of joy."

Apart from a brief opening title saying "Glass and a Half Full Production" in white on a Cadbury purple background, the only branding in the entire 90 seconds is the 5-second tag at the end. Yet that video was a resounding marketing, image rebuilding, and sales success. The impact of the video was so great that Todd Stitzer, Cadbury's CEO at the time, called 2007 "The Year of the Gorilla."

Both T-Mobile and Cadbury have recognized the strength of light branding, and they have successfully repeated that formula again and again with videos like *Cadbury Eyebrows* (9.3 million views), *The T-Mobile Welcome Back* (12 million views), and *The T-Mobile Royal Wedding* (26 million views). And they're not the only brands doing it. Sony Bravia has used this same style of light branding in their series of big viral hits including *Balls*, *Paint*, and *Play-Doh*. Stride gum used this sponsorship approach in *Where the Hell Is Matt?*

Links to
These
Examples

2006 (18 million views) and liked it so much, they sponsored the sequel, *Where the Hell Is Matt? 2008* (43 million views), one of our favorite viral videos of all time. We will be forever grateful to Stride for making that video possible.

In video after video, all these companies have repeatedly kept their brand presence very light, just a title card or two at the end saying who made this awesomeness possible. They've seen the results you get when the branding itself doesn't interfere with the contagiousness. That's important.

But Does It Move Product?

Traditional advertising pros may fret over the limited brand presence in these kinds of videos, but only because they don't yet understand the difference between what works online and what works in traditional advertising. Trust us, *light branding moves product.*

Just ask Blendtec. Their CEO (and viral video star) Tom Dickson reports that their sales went up 700 percent as a result of the *Will It Blend?* videos. Those videos put the Blendtec brand on the map. Well-established companies have gotten remarkable results as well.

The *Financial Times* reported that sales for Cadbury's Dairy Milk chocolate bars spiked by 9 percent in the two months after the video was released and were up 4 to 5 percent for the year. And according to a case study by T-Mobile's online partner Unruly Media, *The T-Mobile Dance* generated not just extraordinary word of mouth for the company but it also contributed to a 22 percent sales uplift for T-Mobile handsets.

In our first two Coke and Mentos viral video hits, we worked hard to eliminate every unnecessary product shot, yet using that light branding approach, both of those videos generated sales spikes of more than 5 percent in U.S. sales of two-liter bottles of Diet Coke. Sales of Mentos in the United States jumped 15 percent for the year in just three months.

Our videos generated those kinds of sales because they went viral. Tens of millions of people watched them and liked them so much that they passed them on to their friends. And sales shot up. But if those videos had been saddled with traditional logo and product shots, they wouldn't have gone viral, no one would have seen them, and they would have had no effect on sales.

Approach your branding with a very light touch the way we did with Coke and Mentos, the way T-Mobile, Cadbury, Sony, Stride, and others have done, and your work has a chance to go viral and carry your message to millions. Approach it the way traditional marketers do, however, and your hopes to go viral will likely be dead on arrival.

Be Unforgettable

The essential is to excite the spectators. If that means playing
Hamlet on a flying trapeze or in an aquarium, you do it.

—ORSON WELLES

In order to be contagious, to get us excited enough to
share with our friends, your video has to be, in some way,
unforgettable.

Take a look at *Time* magazine's list of the top 50 YouTube
videos of all time. The top 10 are these:

- *Charlie Bit My Finger—Again!*
- *Evolution of Dance*
- *David After Dentist*
- *OK Go—Here It Goes Again* (treadmills)
- *RickRoll'D*
- *Leave Britney Alone!*
- *University of Florida Student Tasered at
  Kerry Forum*, a.k.a. *Don't Tase Me, Bro!*
- *Charlie Schmidt's Keyboard Cat!—THE
  ORIGINAL!*
- *Dramatic Chipmunk*
- *Hitler's Downfall*

Links to
These
Examples

As different as all of these are from each other, each of them gives us a moment of something unforgettable. Other top 10 lists teach exactly the same lesson. For example, the British *Sun* newspaper's top 10 are these:

- *Charlie Bit My Finger—Again!*
- *The Sneezing Baby Panda*
- *Susan Boyle*
- *Evolution of Dance*
- *Best Ever!!! (Kicesie Drew, the "Sexpert" Girl)*
- *Star Wars Kid*
- *Numa Numa*
- *Christian the Lion*
- *Inspired Bicycles*
- *Dramatic Chipmunk*

Links to These Examples

While the *Sun*'s choices are almost entirely different from *Time* magazine's, here too every single one is, in one way or another, unforgettable.

What is it that makes a video unforgettable?

Videos that go viral show us something we've never seen before. Susan Boyle isn't just another singer. We've never seen anyone like her before. She's a great singer in an unlikely package. That's both odd and inspiring, which is an almost perfect recipe for going viral.

Something unforgettable—something new and exciting—is exactly what makes for good sideshow. In fact, most of the videos on these lists could be easily translated into sideshow acts that could have a long and successful life on Coney Island.

Like sideshow acts, unforgettable content comes in all shapes and sizes. It can be as breathtaking and dramatic as the crocodile versus lions versus buffalo free-for-all in *Battle at Kruger* or as small and inconsequential as the handheld video of a baby monkey hitching a ride on the back of a pig in *Baby Monkey (Going Backwards on a Pig)*. It can be as complex as the 19-stage Rube Goldberg machine Joseph Herscher created to turn a single page of his morning newspaper for *The Page Turner* (6.7 million views) or as simple as two people sitting at a table performing a dance with nothing but their hands like Suzanne Cleary and Peter Harding did in *We No Speak Americano ft. Cleary & Harding* (8.8 million views).

Links to
These
Examples

Unforgettable videos can be as serious as the relentless barrage of facts that come at us in *Did You Know?* (15 million views) or as trivial and frivolous as a five-second clip of a pet prairie dog turning his head toward the camera to a cheesy adventure movie soundtrack in the (slightly inaccurately titled) *Dramatic Chipmunk* (36 million views). What all of these wildly different videos have in common is that they're each unforgettable.

You can even be unforgettable by being bad. *Friday—Rebecca Black* (200+ million views) is an auto-tuned vanity music video made by Ark Music Factory starring then-13-year-old Rebecca Black. It is so bad that it received over 3.1 million "dislikes" in the first three months it was online. *Friday* is a reminder that unforgettable doesn't always come from being great.

Friday—
Rebecca
Black

There are many different ways to make a video that is unforgettable, from being the biggest or the best to being unusual or even laughably bad, yet most attempts at viral video fail because they fall short of this goal.

When you're making your video, don't stop searching for material until you've found the stunt, the person, the reaction, the cat, the rant, the song, the skill, or the something odd that will make your video unforgettable. Show us something new and exciting—that's the strongest tactic for going viral.

Be Resourceful

Don't give up. If you think creatively, you can come up with something unforgettable with whatever you've got at hand. Consider *Thriller (original upload)* (51 million views), an homage to Michael

Jackson's classic 1983 *Thriller* music video and perhaps one of the most intriguing viral videos ever posted to YouTube.

Thriller

Thriller was created by over 1,500 inmates locked behind the walls of the maximum security Cebu Provincial Detention and Rehabilitation Center in the Philippines. In 2007, with the permission and support of the prison superintendent Byron Garcia, over 1,500 inmates took to the prison yard and performed an epic, tightly choreographed dance. Though the Cebu prisoners' choreography is somewhat different than Jackson's original *Thriller* video, the inmates' mass performance is so precise and well done that many viewers assumed they must have copied Jackson's video step for step. The image of so many prisoners, all but one clad in identical prison-issue orange pants and T-shirts, dancing with such artistry and professionalism, is such a break from what we usually expect to see from prison inmates that the video of the event was unforgettable and went viral almost immediately.

The Cebu *Thriller* video is remarkable for how many factors make it unforgettable. A video of over 1,500 people dancing to *Thriller*—that's a good idea. But this isn't just any group of people. It's inmates in a maximum security prison. Now we're talking unforgettable. Then it turns out they have really choreographed the heck out of the piece, and they all really can dance. *Dramatic Chipmunk* has one idea and a silly but unforgettable five seconds. *Thriller* has a lot going for it that adds up to an unforgettable four and a half minutes.

Like *Thriller*, you, too, can aim for a combination of different factors to be unforgettable. The action, the circumstances, the setting, the size, the emotion—all of these can contribute to making your video unforgettable. And like our four rules for being contagious, the more you add, the better chance you have at creating something special.

Unforgettable: The Bar Is High but Achievable

To get people sharing, you have to offer them something new and exciting that they won't easily forget. But you don't have to come up with something life changing. You only need to create something that is unusual enough to stick in memory.

David After Dentist surely isn't going to change anyone's life, but the innocence and earnestness of poor, bewildered David, having trouble comprehending that his reality is still warped by the residual effects of the anesthesia he's just been given, is different from anything we've ever seen. And at the same time, it touches just enough of our emotions to be unforgettable.

Susan Boyle, Star Wars Kid, and *Don't Tase Me, Bro!* are unforgettable in completely different ways from the ways a Yosemite waterfall, the Pyramids of Giza, or the Eiffel Tower are unforgettable, but they are each odd enough in their own sideshow ways to stick in our memory long after we've seen them, and that quality is key to making them contagious.

When *you* begin creating your own videos, aim for content that's different. Aim for content that stands out from the crowd. Aim for something mind-blowing. Aim for something weird. When you do that, you'll be on track to having something unforgettable enough to go viral.

CHAPTER 10

Do Something Different

Bike Lanes

Your job is to create something unforgettable. How do you do that?

The place to start is the sideshow. Approaching this as the twenty-first-century sideshow, you see right away that it's the odd, unusual, weird, and obsessive that stand out as unforgettable. The Internet rewards bold and crazy choices. Rebecca Black's *Friday* was passed around because it was so oddly bad. Before that, Tay Zonday's *Chocolate Rain* had similar success because, although Zonday can indeed sing, his video had such a weird vibe to it that it was hard to forget.

Look at Charlie Schmidt's *Keyboard Cat* (25 million views) or Chris Crocker's over-the-top tearful rant in *Leave Britney Alone!* video (44 million views). Both are direct descendants of centuries of well-established sideshow tradition. The intentionally weird and androgynous Chris Crocker has cultivated an extreme persona, and

Leave
Britney
Alone!

his absurd, weepy complaining about something as inconsequential as tabloid coverage of Britney Spears created an unforgettable freak show moment that is hard to get out of your head.

In the same way, *Keyboard Cat* combined classic sideshow elements of a trained animal act with a generous dose of "That can't be real, how are they faking it?" appeal that traces its roots back at least to P. T. Barnum and Moses Kimball's Fiji Mermaid (the taxidermy masterpiece created from the stuffed torso and head of a juvenile monkey sewn to the bottom half of the stuffed body of a fish) and on through the mysterious mythical jackalope of tourist trap infamy. Like the Fiji Mermaid and the jackalope, *Keyboard Cat* creates a surprisingly effective illusion that, while not entirely convincing, is not easily dismissed at first.

Both *Keyboard Cat* and *Leave Britney Alone!* presented something new, bold, and unabashedly weird, and that approach was a crucial factor in their success.

In a similar vein, take a look at what Tim Street has done with his *French Maid TV* videos. Teaching CPR online? Useful. Important.

French
Maid TV

Boring. But Tim Street's sideshow of barely dressed French maids teaching CPR? That's different.

That got over half a million views, and his *French Maid TV* channel on YouTube has had over 13 million. True, a little sex appeal didn't hurt either. In that way, sideshow, the Internet, film, and television are pretty much the same. (However, some of *French Maid TV* has the potential disadvantage of having been flagged on YouTube as "inappropriate for some viewers," which may have reduced the view counts since people have to navigate the age verification barriers.)

So, is your idea different enough? Try to imagine the carnival barker's pitch for it. When it's as compelling as "Step right up! Step right up! See a cat play a song on a keyboard!" you've probably got something.

Don't Go Halfway

When you try to be different, don't go halfway. When Sun Products' "All" brand "Small and Mighty" laundry detergent wanted to venture into viral video, the company spared no expense. The producers partnered with the hit television show *Celebrity Apprentice*, and they had *Celebrity Apprentice* head honcho Donald Trump assign the two competing teams on the show the task of creating a viral video for "Small and Mighty." The brand also had its own creative agency make a video featuring *Celebrity Apprentice* competitors. Company marketing executives would then choose which of the three candidates—the two created by the competing *Celebrity Apprentice* teams and the one from All's ad agency—to release online.

The winner chosen by All's marketing executives was the video created by the ad agency: a game show send-up called *Guess That Stain!* starring comedienne Joan Rivers.

Guess That
Stain!

Sadly, despite the budget, *Guess That Stain!* was singularly forgettable. The premise was exactly what one might guess from the title, and the "game" wasn't even a real game but a weak and clearly scripted (that is, not *true*) parody of one. The stains that the actors playing "contestants" had to "guess" the origins of were the most run-of-the-mill stains imaginable: relish, ketchup, and root beer for round 1; salad dressing, barbecue sauce, and mouthwash for round 2. The two players stayed put at their game show–style podiums the entire time, and they never got near the stains to touch, smell, or otherwise interact with them. So, while the stains themselves could have been entertainingly different, the timid producers of the piece chose to keep them ordinary.

Had the company taken a true sideshow approach to this—for example, blindfolding the players and making them guess by smell or texture and giving them freakish sideshow stains like elephant boogers or monkey diaper—*that* video might have gone somewhere.

The concept for *Guess That Stain!* has any number of wild and unforgettable possibilities built into it, and All could have done something different enough to be memorable. But a game show where the goal is to stand at a podium and guess which stain is barbecue sauce and which is root beer? That's a tough sell on the Internet or anywhere else.

Despite the draw of a celebrity host like Joan Rivers and the impressive amount of network television time within the *Celebrity Apprentice* program itself that effectively promoted the project to millions of Americans, *Guess That Stain!* generated a total of only 2,600 views online.

Guess That Stain! failed by not going far enough. There was an original and contagious idea waiting to happen. But All just didn't dare to be different. Blendtec's Internet classic *Will It Blend?* series has a similar premise, but unlike All, Blendtec took things far enough to be so weird and different that their videos are extremely contagious. Instead of showing Blendtec blenders making smoothies, they blend iPhones, glow sticks, and marbles. That's being different.

Will It
Blend?

Don't let your ideas stop in safe, boring territory like *Guess That Stain!* Push them to be different.

Remember to think about your sideshow pitch. Is it, "Step right up! Step right up! See an actor try to identify a ketchup stain!" Or is it, "Step right up! Step right up! See a guy put golf balls in a blender!" One is contagious. One is not.

Different Doesn't Have to Be Gross

People often think of different as meaning you have to be crazy like Chris Crocker, edgy like *French Maid TV*, or gross like trying to identify a stain made by elephant boogers. But different can also be friendly, like our Coke and Mentos videos or *Keyboard Cat*. Those have great sideshow pitches as well.

How about this: "Step right up! Watch a man crash his bicycle again and again into New York City traffic just to make a point!" It's not a bad hook, and it perfectly describes *Bike Lanes by Casey Neistat* (5.6 million views), which YouTube's trends manager Kevin Allocca points to as an example of a video

Bike Lanes

that went viral because it included moments that were unexpected. And indeed it does. But it's not just unexpected. It's more than that: it's unforgettable.

Neistat's video starts with what looks like cell phone camera footage of a New York City cop writing him a ticket for riding his bike outside the designated bike lane—something that, it turns out, is *not* actually illegal in New York City. Unaware at that point that the law he is being ticketed for breaking does not even apply in the city, Neistat tries to explain to the cop that bikes often have to avoid the bike lane because New York bike lanes are so often dangerously obstructed. The cop is unmoved.

A music track then begins to play, and the video continues with footage of Neistat riding his bike *in* the bike lane while talking to the camera about the problem of bike lane obstructions. Before he can quite finish making his point, he crashes spectacularly into a wall of construction barriers blocking the bike path. The video then cuts to seven more increasingly dramatic collisions between a biking Neistat and a variety of dangerous obstructions in the bike lane, including, pointedly, a New York City police cruiser, into which Neistat smashes gloriously.

After the second crash, we begin to suspect that the collisions are staged, and if we're still undecided, the collision with a furniture delivery truck that sends Neistat flying off his bike and vaulting nimbly into the back of an open delivery truck makes it pretty clear. Surprisingly, however, the change from cinema verité to a bike-riding-and-stunt-crashing video that's a first cousin to Danny MacAskill's bike trick videos doesn't bother us because the stunts themselves are real and well executed, and they indelibly make

Neistat's point that bike lanes in New York City are constantly fraught with hazards.

The combination of the surprise when Neistat first smashes into the construction barriers almost midsentence and tumbles to the asphalt and the almost comedic stunt crashes that follow created a video that made his point so clearly that those who have seen it will likely never forget that (1) you can get a $50 ticket in New York City for not riding in the bike lane and (2) if you do ride your bike just in the bike lanes in New York City, you will crash.

So as you begin to craft your own work in the hopes that it will go viral, look at what's already out there. Then, like Casey Neistat, do something different, something weird, something no one has ever seen before.

What's *your* booth in the twenty-first-century sideshow going to be?

CHAPTER 11

Own It

Inspired Bicycles

If you have an odd idea, something different, that can sometimes be enough, but the way to make something truly unforgettable is to take that idea and make it yours. Own it.

Your goal is to show us something we've never seen before. Often that means you need to show us something that's the best of its kind—on the planet. That was the key to making videos like *Greyson Chance Singing Paparazzi* (48 million views), Levi's *Guys Backflip into Jeans* (8 million views), and even *Dude Transports 22 Bricks on His Head* (1.9 million views) viral hits.

When we say "own it," we mean take whatever intrigues you, a simple idea or a complex one, and take it far enough so that it's *your* territory. Sand artists Ilana Yahav and Kseniya Simonova, for example, created beautiful images simply by spreading sand on a light table or overhead projector. They've

Links to
These
Examples

mastered that medium. They own it. The richness of the images these artists can produce with nothing but sand and light is breathtaking, so it's no surprise that Ilana Yahav's video *Sand Art by Ilana Yahav, SandFantasy, "You've Got a Friend"* has had 4.3 million views on YouTube.

Sand Art by Ilana Yahav

Sometimes owning it means putting in a lifetime of practice. Danny MacAskill has spent so much of his life on a bike that, as he told Carol Wallace of the *New York Times*, "I am more comfortable on my bike than I am on my feet." MacAskill is one of the world's great stunt bicycle riders, and his videos show it.

But few of us can ride a bike like Danny MacAskill. If we could, his videos wouldn't affect us the way they do. So what do the rest of us do to create video that's unforgettable?

Becoming Unforgettable

It turns out that there are two paths to becoming the best in the world. The most common, and the hardest, is the path Danny MacAskill took. Take something we all know, like riding a bicycle, and work tirelessly at it until you have surpassed all those who've gone before you. That was Roger Bannister's breaking the four-minute mile, or Rocky Marciano's winning all 49 fights of his entire professional career.

But there's another path too, and it's the path we like to take: do something almost no one has ever tried before. If you're trying to break the record for a mile run, you've got a lot of competition, but when you're going into an area that's relatively unexplored, you can often get to unforgettable territory a lot more quickly. Matt McAllister, for example, did this with a time-lapse video showing an odd stunt that was far off the beaten path. He donned T-shirt after T-shirt after T-shirt until he was wearing 155 of them at once—a Guinness World Record for T-shirt wearing. We didn't even know Guinness had such a category, but "owning" extreme

T-shirt wearing earned McAllister 17 million views online.

Most
T-Shirts
Worn at
One Time

But be careful. Even something as seemingly innocuous as this can be difficult and
even dangerous. In 2009, Matt McAllister
tried to break the T-shirt record again. When he got to the 177th
shirt—well short of the new record of 227—the pressure on his chest
and lungs became so great that he had to be cut out of them and
given oxygen. Shortly thereafter, McAllister wisely announced that
he was retiring from the world of extreme T-shirt wearing.

If you're working on something few people have ever tried before,
you can become the best in the world in a remarkably short time.
That's what we did with Coke and Mentos. When we first started to
work with soda and candy geysers, there were already scores of Coke
and Mentos videos on the Internet. All of them were essentially the
same: a couple of guys firing a single-bottle geyser into the air in a
random suburban driveway.

We tried it ourselves just for fun, and we were so taken with
the phenomenon that we had to dig into it and figure out what
more there might be. We weren't sure what we'd find, but within
24 hours, we had put together a choreographed 10-bottle geyser
display. We performed it that night at the Oddfellow Theater in our
hometown of Buckfield, Maine, one of the theaters where we often
test out new ideas. The piece was a hit with the Oddfellow Theater
audience, and we knew almost immediately that we had to explore
it more deeply and work to take it all the
way to unforgettable.

Our First,
Very Rough
Coke and
Mentos
Performance

Pretty much every Saturday for the
next five months, Stephen drove up from
his house in Massachusetts to Fritz's juggling studio in Maine, and we worked
all weekend to learn everything we could about Coke and Mentos.
We compared different sodas, we compared diet versus regular, we
drilled holes in the sides of bottles, and we swung spraying geysers
around our heads on ropes. Much of what we tried didn't work

(Fritz swinging a geyser around himself on a rope, while getting sprayed by it the entire time stands out as a particularly entertaining failure), but what did work turned into *The Extreme Diet Coke & Mentos Experiments*.

That video went viral because it was unforgettable, and it was unforgettable in large part because we took a simple idea and owned it. We took it further than any sane person would. That video demonstrated, in a true, human, and unapologetically silly way, the lengths to which we had gone in exploring what could be done with Coke and Mentos geysers, and people really got a kick out of that.

The takeaway for you is that by the time we shot that video, we had, without doubt, become the world's foremost authorities on something very odd.

How do you become the world's greatest at something in a short amount of time? It's hard if you want to be a world-class juggler or a concert violinist, but it's not if your chosen field is one that has never before been explored. We became the world experts in a matter of months, working only on weekends. You can too. The Coke and Mentos combination has now been extensively explored, but the world of unexplored niches that you can master is infinite.

A Repeatable Formula

You can do this. We've used this approach time and again. It's repeatable.

For our video *The Extreme Sticky Note Experiments*, we followed the same process, only with sticky notes. While playing with sticky notes to see what potential they might have for a video, we discovered the sticky note pads made for pop-up dispensers that are stuck together in zigzag fashion. We found that this kind of pad can act like a Slinky and can create a beautiful colored-paper waterfall. With that as a start, we began to explore how far we could take it, and a few months later, we had once again become world experts, this time in the tiny, little explored field of sticky note waterfalls.

The same process got us to the Coke and Mentos–powered rocket car. We knew that Coke and Mentos could push a skateboard, but what would owning it look like? Pushing a human. Just as it did with sticky notes, it just took steady work toward that goal. The results? Both our sticky note video and rocket car video have had over 4 million views online and tens of millions of people saw us re-create them on *Letterman*, *Good Morning America*, and more.

So while creating something unforgettable by owning it can take work, you can do it. From our crazy experiments to Judson Laipply's *Evolution of Dance* to OK Go's videos with treadmills, chain reactions, and dog tricks, setting out to own it is achievable and rewarding. Each of these examples finds a quirky idea where it won't take too long to achieve something unforgettable.

For Judson Laipply, that meant working continually on improving and adding to his dance mashup over the course of a few years. For us with Coke and Mentos, it meant working weekends for a few months. For Matt McAllister, his T-shirt record probably took a week or so to organize.

As you work to take your idea all the way to this level, there are also a few specific strategies that you can use to get beyond what everyone else is doing and own it.

Strategy 1: Do It Until You Get It

An important strategy for owning it on video is being willing to take the time to shoot take after take after take to get just the right shot.

Danny MacAskill's bicycle riding is a world-class stunt act, but his videos are unforgettable because he combines that world-class skill with the dogged persistence to shoot again and again until he gets the footage he wants. To get the shot of his amazing ride across the spiked top of a wrought iron fence, MacAskill and his videographer Dave Sowerby spent four days of shooting just to get 15 seconds of footage. Recognize that, even when you're as good as MacAskill, you might not get something unforgettable on the first take. Or the second. Or the tenth.

OK Go's treadmill dance took 17 takes to get it right. Their *White Knuckles* video with all those dogs took them 124 takes—and the "dogamid" dog pyramid at the end came out just right in only 2, but when they got it, they had gold.

So just as you need to be persistent in exploring the niche in which you're going to become the world's greatest, you may need to be equally persistent when it comes time to shoot your video. You may not own it on the first take.

Strategy 2: Scale It Up

As Oscar Wilde reminded us, "Nothing succeeds like excess." When you need to own it in a way no one ever has before, scale is your friend. As you explore, if you're intrigued by 1 of something, ask yourself what would happen if you had 100 of them. That's what we did for *The Extreme Diet Coke & Mentos Experiments*. Then ask what would happen if you had 250,000—which is what we did for *The Extreme Sticky Note Experiments*.

Your idea can become something different, something memorable, when you introduce scale.

Sony
Bravia's
Balls

The folks from Sony Bravia and their agency Fallon created a great example of pure scale at work in their *Balls* video, taking the simple idea of a ball bouncing down a hill and owning it by scaling the idea up. To see 1 ball bouncing down a hill: that's not so different. But 250,000 balls bouncing down a hill in San Francisco? Owning it.

In exploring your ideas, in figuring out how it is that you're going to own the niche you're exploring, always consider what it might be like to introduce scale. For the folks at Sony, that was all they needed.

Similarly, there were dozens of Coke and Mentos videos already online when we first began to explore the phenomenon, but it was 100 geysers choreographed into an absurdly huge production number that made *The Extreme Diet Coke & Mentos Experiments* go viral. After we'd first experimented with 10, we thought, "Let's do 40—that would be crazy!" Soon, it was 50. Then 60. Eventually, we realized that we needed to do 100. That would be *owning it*.

From *The Extreme Diet Coke & Mentos Experiments* to the hand dance in Up and Over It's *We No Speak Americano* to Sony Bravia's *Balls* to OK Go's videos, going beyond what anyone else has done before has created some unforgettable videos. To make your video unforgettable, find something you can take further than anyone else has. Run with your raw idea as far as you can.

Whatever quirky niche you've chosen, explore it until you know it completely. Then ramp it up even more, and *don't stop until you own it*. If you have to, try it again and again until you get that unforgettable shot. And always consider scaling it up and making it really big. Take it to your own *Extreme Diet Coke & Mentos Experiments*, your own *Sand Art* or your own *Evolution of Dance*. That's the kind of thinking that makes videos go viral.

CHAPTER 12

Capture a Unique Moment

Frozen Grand Central

The more you can give people a one-of-a-kind experience, the better. Sometimes those moments are planned, sometimes they are spontaneous, but they're most contagious when they are unique.

If you can catch footage of a battle in the wild between a pack of lions, a herd of water buffalo and a crocodile, or if you can have your camera rolling when a baby panda sneezes, you've got something. Laughing babies are good subjects for this kind of video (*Laughing Baby* [5.8 million views] is just one of many), but confused toddlers appear to rule all others. *David After Dentist* (110 million views) and *Charlie Bit My Finger*, for example, show us kids in one-of-a-kind candid moments that have made for some of the most highly contagious videos of all time.

To get this kind of video, sometimes you have to be in exactly the right place at exactly the right time, and that can make people think that trying to create a viral video is like trying to catch lightning in a bottle and you just have to be lucky. But while luck can help, you can create your own.

Creating Your Own Luck

If you're not lucky enough to have caught something like *David After Dentist* or *Battle at Kruger* on video, what do you do? How do you set out to create a video of a unique moment?

One tactic is to create a situation in which something true, human, and unforgettable is likely to happen and then make sure your camera is rolling when it does. Matt Harding did this in *Where the Hell Is Matt? 2008.* He went out and filmed himself doing a silly little dance in places like in a field of tulips in the Netherlands, on the edge of the crashing surf in Tonga, and for contrast, in front of a humorless guard in the demilitarized zone between North and South Korea. He caught the moment when the surf in Tonga crashed right over him. He caught the priceless, stony-faced reaction of the guard. For each shot, Matt Harding created the circumstances for something unique to happen, and it did. Those unforgettable moments help make his video so contagious.

Where the Hell Is Matt? 2008

Charlie Todd's Improv Everywhere also goes out into the world and creates unique moments. Improv Everywhere's flash mob stunts create bizarre situations, and their videos capture people's candid reactions. Charlie Todd told us that he believes that one of the key reasons for his success is that "the Internet has an appetite for things that really happened in real life." Like Matt Harding, Improv Everywhere creates real life situations in which it's likely that something interesting will happen.

In *Frozen Grand Central* (31 million views), 207 Improv Everywhere "agents" showed up in the main lobby of Grand Central Terminal separately, as though they didn't know each other, and at a predetermined time, all of them froze in place. It was as if they had become 207 human statues. They stayed frozen like that for five full minutes. When the time was up, they resumed what they had been doing as though nothing unusual had happened. The reactions of people seeing all this happen are viral video gold. The commuters and other passersby wandered through the "statues," touching them, taking pictures, questioning what on Earth was going on.... Those unique, candid moments added up to tens of millions of views online.

Frozen Grand Central

No Pants Subway Ride

For Improv Everywhere's annual *No Pants Subway Ride*, their "agents" dress normally except for one thing: they "forget" their pants and ride the New York City subway. The eighth annual ride involved over 1,200 "agents," and the video of the event—showing people's funny reactions to it—got 19 million views on YouTube. All told, Improv Everywhere's videos have had over 230 million views. All from creating unusual circumstances and capturing them on film.

Candid Camera

The idea of secretly watching people's reactions to bizarre, set-up situations has no doubt been a staple of entertainment since the days of the prehistoric cave dwellers, but the patriarch of making secret recordings of those reactions and presenting them to an audience was Allen Funt.

During World War II, a young Funt was assigned to the Army Signal Corps and was posted to a base in Oklahoma. Reading the "gripe" column in the Army newspaper *Yank* one day, Funt decided to try to record soldiers' complaints about life in the service and edit those complaints together into a feature for Armed Forces Radio.

When he was done recording, however, he discovered that the microphones and recording equipment had made the soldiers stiff and self-conscious and that the resulting piece was flat and boring. The voices of the men Funt recorded didn't sound like soldiers did when they really complained. They didn't sound *true*.

Funt realized that what he needed were real, spontaneous complaints, not staged readings into a microphone. He set out again. This time he concealed his microphones and recorded real soldiers actually griping in real-life situations. The results were hilarious.

When Funt got out of the army, he remembered the success he'd had with the secret recordings, tweaked the idea a bit, and turned it into a radio show he called *Candid Microphone*, which debuted on ABC Radio in 1947. Rather than record complaints from service members, Funt set up crazy scenarios in the real world and recorded ordinary people reacting to them. *Candid Microphone* launched with a scene in which Funt hired a sign painter and, with a straight face, asked the painter to paint his own name, Lester Cannon, on Funt's office door, all the while secretly recording the conversation with the puzzled Mr. Cannon on a hidden wire recorder.

When recording equipment became more portable, Funt moved his pranks from the office out into the world where public parks, candy stores, and dentists' offices became his base of operations. *Candid Microphone* was so successful it moved to television in 1948 as the now-famous *Candid Camera*. Allen Funt's frugally produced *Candid Camera* became one of the longest running shows in television history, and it aired in one form or another for over half a century until it finally wound down in 2004.

Candid Camera's pranks were harmless and fun. Funt would remove the engine from a car, tow the car to the top of a hill, and have his actress sit in the driver's seat while it coasted downhill into a service station where, with hidden camera rolling, she would ask the mechanic to see if he could figure out "why the car was acting up."

Funt would fill an elevator with people all facing the wrong way and then film the reactions as new people got on (or didn't).

From the moment in 1947 when he realized his studio recordings of griping soldiers rang false, Funt understood that the key to success in this kind of work was, as he later put it, simply "to catch people in the act of being themselves."

Funt's success with *Candid Microphone* and later with *Candid Camera* grew out of many of the same sensibilities, the same elements, and the same aesthetic that are the core of what it takes to be successful in online video today. Although there were actors who were in on the pranks, the people on whom the jokes were played were ordinary and unsuspecting, so the pieces were true. Since the essence of each segment was to "catch people in the act of being themselves," they were quite consciously all about humanity. Funt's production techniques were simple. It was cinema verité, shot in real, unglamorous, everyday locations. Like a good sideshow showman, he spent little time on setup or story and instead quickly got down to the business of letting his audience watch real people reacting to the unusual situations he had created. And the strange, surreal situations Funt constructed often made for moments that were unforgettable. Who could ever forget lifting the hood of a car to see what might be wrong, only to discover there was no engine at all? Or the time the elevator door opened and the 11 people inside were all facing the back wall? Could you ever forget seeing that happen to someone else?

What Allen Funt started in the 1940s with *Candid Microphone* and *Candid Camera* has continued in various forms on television right up through the long running *TV's Bloopers and Practical Jokes* and *Totally Hidden Video,* on into Ashton Kutcher's edgier *Punk'd.*

NBC's *Tonight Show* has had great success both on TV and online with its *Tonight Show Photo Booth,* in which an "automatic" free photo booth is set up inside of Universal Studios to lure passing tourists. Inside the booth, what seems like a computerized voice gives people instructions, but it's really the voice of comedienne Kira Soltanovich, who can see everything that's going on and has fun telling the tourists what they "must"

Tonight Show Photo Booth

do to get their pictures taken. View counts for the photo booth on NBC.com aren't made public, but even one of the unofficial copies on YouTube has upward of 2.8 million views.

Online, the king of Funt's *Candid Camera*–style technique is French viral video hitmaker Rémi Gaillard. His offbeat pranks and hidden camera videos have garnered a total of over *1 billion* views online. And all of his work harkens back directly to the *Candid Camera* and *Candid Microphone* work of Allen Funt. Indeed, some of Gaillard's videos look like they could have been created by Funt himself. In Gaillard's *Everest Elevator* (4.1 million views), for example, he surprises a woman waiting for an elevator. When the elevator doors part, there

Everest
Elevator

Foot
Elevator

is no elevator car at all, only Gaillard clad in full mountain climbing gear, hanging on a rope, scaling the elevator shaft as if it were the Matterhorn. Similarly, in *Foot Elevator* (5.5 million views), Gaillard surprises another unsuspecting woman when the doors to her elevator open to reveal a fully furnished, if somewhat cramped, mini-studio apartment with Galliard sitting on a lounge chair, watching television, apparently irritated by the interruption.

All of Galliard's work takes a classic *Candid Camera* approach. In *Mister Universe* (25 million views), Gaillard crashes the Mr. Universe bodybuilding competition. Clad only in his underwear, he

Mister
Universe

roams around, stretches, does pushups, and attempts to blend in with the heavily oiled, tanned, and overly ripped, thong-wearing competitors. The contrast between the fit, but pale and normal-bodied, Gaillard and the bizarrely muscled Mr. Universe competitors is both amusing and a thought-provoking commentary on the world of bodybuilding.

While capturing a unique moment like *David After Dentist* or *Battle at Kruger* requires some luck, Rémi Gaillard doesn't rely on luck to get his 1 billion views.

When you're looking to capture a unique moment, you have some strategies available to you. You can go out and create simple, candid moments, as Matt Harding does in his *Where the Hell Is Matt?* videos, or you can create surreal circumstances, like Improv Everywhere and Rémi Gaillard do, and watch people react.

As Allen Funt discovered back in the 1940s, you can find something unforgettable by setting up a slightly bizarre situation and catching people "in the act of being themselves."

CHAPTER 13

FOR MARKETERS:
Be Bold Enough
to Be Unforgettable

Cadbury Gorilla

Being unforgettable means going out on a limb and trying something different. That can seem risky.

But the real risk in online video is in trying to play it safe. If you're not different enough to distance yourself from the pack, your video won't go viral and your entire effort will have been wasted. If your target demographic doesn't find your video unforgettable, they won't care and they won't share, so don't put your budget into television-style production techniques. Put it into making something unforgettable. *That's* where you'll see the return.

Are you bold enough to do that? Is your boss bold enough? Your legal department?

Cadbury has been great at this, creating unforgettable videos with a drumming gorilla and an odd but captivating eyebrow dance. Both videos went out on a creative limb and brought them phenomenal success.

After the success of the boldly unusual *Cadbury Gorilla* drumming to Phil Collins's "In the Air Tonight," Cadbury was daring

Cadbury Eyebrows

enough to create something weirdly different and hugely successful again with *Cadbury Eyebrows*, in which a boy and a girl sit in a photographer's studio preparing to have their portrait taken. When the photographer steps out for a moment, the boy presses a button on his watch, which then starts playing the song "Don't Stop the Rock" by Freestyle. As the music plays from the watch, the two kids proceed to raise, lower, and ripple their eyebrows in an elaborate eyebrow dance in time to the music. After a minute of enjoying this classic sideshow-style stunt, this video also fades to the brand message: "Cadbury Dairy Milk, a glass and a half full of joy." *Eyebrows* was another bold campaign, and that boldness has paid off with 9.3 million views online.

Cadbury Trucks

Between *Gorilla* and *Eyebrows*, however, Cadbury had made the mistake of playing it safe. They created *Cadbury Trucks*, a video of airport baggage trucks speeding around an airport. No crashes, no accidents, no stunts, no one injured—in fact, no humans visible at all.

Perhaps there was the germ of an idea there that could have been different enough to catch on online, but without more, it wasn't enough. The most popular YouTube copy we were able to find has had only 360,000 views.

Cadbury Trucks makes several mistakes, but most of all, it just doesn't have that sideshow hook. Step right up, step right up, see... uh, baggage trucks racing around an empty airport? It appears Cadbury learned its lesson from that video, however, and it came back strong with the much bolder, odder, and far more successful *Cadbury Eyebrows*.

The guys at Blendtec went out on a limb to show their powerful kitchen blenders doing what they aren't supposed to do: blending everything from an iPhone to glowsticks to golf balls. Their classic *Will It Blend?* series has more than 50 videos that each has had over 1 million views.

Will It
Blend?

Seeing a blender violently shred an iPhone into bits of metal and black powder is unforgettable. We're perhaps a bit worried for the safety of the guy doing it, but it's a fantastic hook. And suddenly Blendtec is the coolest blender on the planet. Before *Will It Blend?*, who thought a blender could be cool?

It's easy to imagine the head of Blendtec getting a memo from his legal department saying, "We don't want to appear to be encouraging people to put cell phones, hockey pucks, and tablet computers in our blenders." But if legal had shut down *Will It Blend?*, we never would have had the priceless experience of watching a blender shred Justin Bieber's autobiography (1.9 million views).

And Blendtec sales wouldn't have gone up 700 percent the way they did.

Yes, evaluate the risks. Be smart. But if you start by looking only for ideas that are safe, your videos will sink into the oblivion of obscurity. People don't share videos that are the same as everything else they've seen.

If you don't open yourself up to the possibility of doing something bold, it's going to be hard to make something contagious.

You have to be bold enough to find something unforgettable.

You Can Be Unforgettable Without Being Crazy

What if your brand has to be more conservative than Cadbury or Blendtec? Well, you don't have to be wild and crazy to be unforgettable.

Take a look at Dove's *Evolution* (15 million views) a stunning video with a profound message.

Evolution

The video begins with a woman sitting in front of a plain gray backdrop while looking straight into the camera. At time-lapse speed, we watch as fashion professionals do her hair and makeup, take her photograph, and, finally, digitally manipulate the image to make her neck longer, her lips fuller, and her eyes bigger.

After 30 seconds of watching the transformation of this woman's face into an idealized image that only vaguely resembles her, the camera pulls back to show the final photograph up on a billboard. Words come up on the screen: "No wonder our perception of beauty is distorted."

It's not bizarre or wacky, but it's still bold and unforgettable. It's effective and beautifully suited to Dove's brand image.

Even safety itself can be made unforgettable if the treatment is bold enough. Sussex Safer Roads was powerful and poetic with their video *Embrace Life—Always Wear Your Seat Belt* (15 million views),

Embrace Life

showing a car crash through slow-motion mime. A man's wife and daughter wrap their arms around him to become the seat belts that keep him safe.

The video goes against the usual scare tactics of driving safety campaigns for a positive message, strong emotional punch, and unforgettable images. That's what viral video is built for.

Like Dove and Sussex Safer Roads, like Sony Bravia's color-themed viral videos and T-Mobile's train station dance, you, too, can take your ideas to the extreme while still being smart, sophisticated, and on-brand.

Think Super Bowl

In American advertising, often the Super Bowl is the only thing that gets marketers thinking this boldly. Is it any wonder that Super Bowl ads are some of the only straight-up commercials that go viral online? They're the ones where marketers take chances and do things that are different.

The Force: Volkswagen Commercial (54 million views) set the bar for a Super Bowl ad going viral online. It's anything but just another car commercial. And, as in any good viral video, the brand presence is integrated and light. Volkswagen branding doesn't even show up until the last few seconds.

The Force

What makes this video unforgettable (at least to everyone who's seen *Star Wars*, which is a lot of people) is watching a little kid dressed as Darth Vader who has spent the day walking around unsuccessfully trying to use the power of the Force on everything from the family dog to a peanut butter and jelly sandwich, until his dad cleverly tricks him into thinking he's really got Jedi powers.

If not for the television commercial production style, this content could be right out of a home movie.

The brand tie-in comes in only at the end, when the boy tries to use the Force on the family's Volkswagen and his dad clicks the remote starter to make the kid think he's succeeded. The boy's incredulous reaction, reeling backward from the car, is priceless.

It's remarkable to think that this video could have been even more powerful. Imagine if it had also followed Rule One, Be True. What if *The Force* really had been a home movie of a dad pranking his son? But that's where a home run in Rule Three, Be Unforgettable, can be the driver of viral spread that overcomes all other failings. We had never seen anything like *The Force* before. That made it powerfully contagious.

So think big. Think bold. Think Super Bowl. Then bring that attitude to the Internet, where you don't have to spend millions and millions of dollars on the Super Bowl ad buy.

Michael Donnelly, then director of interactive marketing at Coca-Cola, said our second viral video for Coca-Cola had "the impact of a Super Bowl ad." You don't get that without being bold.

So don't hold back. When the goal is to be unforgettable, you've got to be open to ideas that dare to be different.

RULE FOUR

Ultimately, It's All About Humanity

We want to look at them because they're different from us, but we keep looking at them because they're the same as us.

—PENN JILLETTE OF PENN & TELLER

More than TV or film, online video has an ability to create a direct, personal connection with its audience, and that intimacy is powerful.

Yes, show us something spectacular. Show us something unforgettable. But above all, show us something human.

The top viral videos all put simple humanity front and center. *Greyson Chance Singing Paparazzi, Numa Numa,* and *Charlie Bit My Finger* just point their cameras at people. We humans seem to like watching other humans like that. It creates an emotional connection that's contagious.

Just about all the successful videos in this book, from *JK Wedding Entrance Dance* to *Soldier Homecoming Surprise Mix* and *Where the Hell Is Matt? 2008,* show us images of humanity that create the strong, positive emotions that make us want to share that experience with our friends.

The smash viral videos from *Britain's Got Talent* showing Susan Boyle, Paul Potts, and Connie Talbot give us just enough setup to deliver a huge payoff when these folks open their mouths to sing. There are other great singers. What makes these videos contagious is the combination of great voices and the humanity on display. Talk about using a sideshow moment to create active, positive emotion that leads to sharing—that's Susan Boyle in a nutshell. Raw, glorious humanity.

Links to These Examples

Show us this kind of humanity in your videos. Don't try to tell human *stories*. Figure out how you can showcase human *moments*. Give us at least one moment of real emotion to connect to. That will go a long way to making your video more contagious.

Also consider turning the camera around to show human *reactions* to extraordinary events. This is what the *Candid Camera*–style videos like *Coca-Cola Happiness Machine* and the videos of Rémi Gaillard and Improv Everywhere are all about. The surprise, the laughter—the genuine human reactions—are Internet gold. When we see the people in the videos smile, we smile too.

America's Funniest Home Videos has run for over 20 years showing humanity, humanity, and more humanity. And people getting hit in the junk.

But really, what is that? Humanity. We can all relate to the genuine pain on display. How many of those same kinds of videos of people hurting themselves have gone viral? More than we would care to count.

From the *Star Wars Kid* who imagines himself in an epic lightsaber battle, to the guy who sits in front of his computer and lip-synchs in *Numa Numa*, we see people being themselves. We see humanity on display. *Numa Numa*, one of the biggest viral hits of all time, is essentially a video of a guy having fun. He's totally unself-conscious as he lip-synchs to a song that makes him happy.

Inspire us to share your video by showing moments of joy like that, even if it's as simple as someone just having a great time lip-synching. Ultimately, that joy is what it's all about. It's all about the humanity.

Human vs. Superhuman

Viral video is the twenty-first-century sideshow, but sideshow and spectacle without an emotional connection is hollow. The best circus and sideshow acts are not about superhumans. They're about humans. If the audience doesn't see the performer as a real person, an act can be amazing but it won't be affecting. Online, it's exactly the same.

Two different videos from Italian foot juggler Selyna Bogino make this point beautifully. In 2011, Bogino put two videos on YouTube showcasing her mind-boggling dexterity with her feet. One went viral.

The first video she posted, *Selyna Bogino—Tigerpalast 2011*, shows her world-class juggling act, performed live in Frankfurt, Germany. It's shot with a single camera from the back of the theater in one uninterrupted take. The curtain opens to show Bogino on a chair in a dramatic pool of light. She's wearing a fedora, tight-fitting Capri pants, and a sparkling, low-cut top. She tosses the fedora offstage, and her act then goes into 40 seconds of dance. We were promised foot juggling, so although her dancing is nice enough, it's wasting our time.

But after the opening dance, Bogino gets down to business and she's amazing. She tosses and catches long cylinders, flipping them end over end using only her feet. She spins four small carpets, one on each hand and one on each foot. Finally, in a remarkable sequence, she throws and catches five basketballs between her hands and feet in a series of creative and jaw-dropping moves. The Tigerpalast audience loves it, and as

Selyna Bogino— Tigerpalast 2011

juggling fans, when we first saw this video, we really enjoyed it too. Her skill is phenomenal.

Then Bogino made a second video, which she describes simply as "practicing at home for fun, to beat the world record of the longest and most difficult 5 balls routine ever…!" *Selyna Bogino Doing the Five Balls Longest Routine Ever! XD* shows her rehearsing in her attic studio. She turns on the single, fixed camera and walks into frame. She's wearing sweatpants and a T-shirt, and behind her is the random assortment of boxes, chairs, and other miscellanea you'd find in any attic.

Selyna Bogino Doing the Five Balls Longest Routine Ever! XD

After a couple brief stretches, she starts right in, doing the same amazing sequence with five basketballs, but now with a few extra, even more astounding tricks. She finishes by tossing the balls onto the floor and tilts her head nonchalantly as she walks up to the camera to turn it off.

It's this video that went viral.

The video of Bogino on stage at the Tigerpalast has had a respectable 44,000 views, but her second video, in which all she was doing was *rehearsing*, got 1.6 million. That view count made it one of the top 10 juggling videos on YouTube to date.

Why did one video go viral and not the other?

Both videos are true. Each documents a real event, with no interference from distracting production tricks.

Both feature unforgettable skills. While the second has a few extra hard tricks, only another juggler would likely notice the difference.

The second video is shorter, and there's no dancing that wastes our time. That's important, but there's an even more fundamental difference.

The first video is dressed up with choreography and a full-on circus costume. Bogino is putting on a big show for us, and on the Tigerpalast stage, she's perfect. That perfection, however, makes her somehow distant, not just physically but emotionally.

The second video is raw. It's just Bogino, her impressive tricks, and her nice-but-ordinary clothes. She's not putting on a big show for us, so we see more of her real self. There, in her attic, she's amazing, but relatable, like someone we might know.

Even though Bogino's rehearsal video doesn't have any over-the-top emotion—she's not elated, she's not jumping up and down, she just gives us a nonchalant tilt of her head—we see the humanity that her polished stage performance hid. And that humanity forges an emotional connection that makes the video contagious.

The more human video creates a stronger emotional connection because it turns out we're more interested in people than in tricks. Selyna Bogino's skill is her reason to make a video. It makes her the person to watch. It helps make her video unforgettable. But in the end, if she's just a plastic superhero whom we can't relate to, we'll have no emotional connection with her. It's when we see her being herself that the viral magic starts to happen.

As you work to create your own unforgettable video, remember to keep the humanity in focus. Keep it real. A video of you in your attic will show more of *you* than an overly packaged performance will. You'll make a stronger emotional connection with your audience by showing us a real human than by showing us a flawless image of a superhuman.

Puppies and Frogs vs. Machines

There's a famous show business saying, sometimes attributed to W. C. Fields: "Never work with children or animals." An adult just can't compete with the audience's instant emotional connection to a child or a puppy. You can see the universal appeal of children in all the laughing baby videos that have millions of views. And sure enough, there are a ton of cute animal videos too.

There are dog videos like *Cute Puppy Falling Asleep* (16 million views), cat videos like *Funny Cats* (17 million views), dog *and* cat videos like *Puppy vs. Cat* (14 million views), and videos of more exotic animals as well, such as *The Sneezing Baby Panda, Battle at Kruger,* and *Porcupine Who Thinks He Is a Puppy!* (2.8 million views). These videos deliver doses of pure emotion. As soon as we click "play," we start empathizing.

Links to These Examples

Watching animals, particularly mammals, can create the same emotional connection that watching people does.

Sometimes, a video doesn't have a human focus. Instead, it has an object focus, like a time-lapse video of a skyscraper going up or a crazy Rube Goldberg machine. For these videos, it helps to find some human element to inject some emotion.

OK Go did a great job of this in their Rube Goldberg machine video for *This Too Shall Pass* (36 million views) by appearing frequently in and around the action without distracting from the cool chain reaction.

Joseph Herscher adds a human element to his machine video too in *The Page Turner* (6.7 million views), which begins by showing Herscher unfolding his newspaper and taking a sip of coffee. Taking that sip of coffee sets off a chain reaction behind him, which, a minute and a half later, turns the page of the newspaper he is reading, whereupon we see Herscher again, nonchalantly taking another sip of coffee. His understated presence in the video helped take what could have been a dry, impersonal video and made it more emotionally engaging, even funny.

The Page Turner   The Way Things Go

One of the greatest Rube Goldberg machines ever built was made by Swiss artists Peter Fischli and the late David Weiss. The machine was documented in *Der Lauf der Dinge (The Way Things Go),* a 30-minute film that shows Fischli and Weiss's fantastic device from start to finish. But the cold, mechanical machinery, imaginative though it is, has no human element, and video of it, while fascinating, is somehow stark and uninviting. Joseph Herscher's *Page Turner* machinery is less impressive, but his more human video has an advantage when it comes to contagiousness.

Sony Bravia, in its video of 250,000 superballs bouncing down a hill in San Francisco, was smart enough to put in shots of a child, a dog, and even a frog, reacting to the colorful bouncing balls. Without those shots—our favorite is the jumping frog—it too could have been just a big, mechanical stunt.

Some of Sony's subsequent videos, like *Pyramids* (330,000 views) and *Domino City* (480,000 views), are less emotional, more mechanical, and not surprisingly, less viral.

Worse than showing no people reacting, however, is showing people *not* reacting. Sony's *Domino City*, which shows real, brightly colored, eight-foot-tall dominoes falling in stunning locations in India, makes the particular mistake of showing images of people who are completely oblivious to the events around them. The fact that these giant dominoes falling make the people around them do and feel nothing tends to make us react the same way.

Pyramids   Domino City

With every video you make, try to include as much pure, simple humanity as you can. Sometimes it'll be just a kid watching all the bouncing balls go by. Other times, it'll be showing the human side of a superhuman, like Selyna Bogino. Or it will simply be a genuine human reaction of joy or pain. Always, you want to find a place where the audience can see themselves, their emotions, or their experiences reflected on the screen. Always, that human element will make your video more contagious.

CHAPTER 14

Give Me the Thrill of Victory and the Agony of Defeat

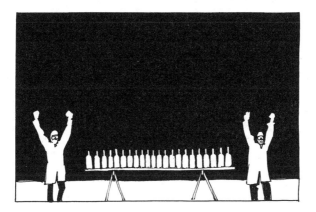

The Extreme Diet Coke & Mentos Experiments

One of the easiest ways to create an emotional connection is to show a moment of success or failure. Show us something unforgettable *and* show us the emotional reaction. That's a contagious combination.

For 37 years, from 1961 through 1998, ABC's *Wide World of Sports* was a television mainstay, and each week it opened with a montage of athletic events accompanied by the iconic voice of broadcaster Jim McKay saying:

> *Spanning the globe... to bring you the constant variety of sport:* the thrill of victory... *and* the agony of defeat... *the human drama of athletic competition.*

As ABC knew, the skill of the athletes it featured each week was world class, but that athleticism alone was not enough to keep viewers coming back week after week. The scores of other sports programs that came and went also had great athletes. What made *Wide World of Sports* such a phenomenal success for so many years was that the producers connected us to the *emotions* of these athletic achievements: the thrill, the agony, the human drama.

Those same emotional moments of success or failure are also what make many viral videos successful. You can see this in action in videos like *FAIL Blog's Frustrated Skateboarder Fail* (4.3 million views), where, after a shirtless kid misses a skateboarding jump, he

Skate-
boarder Fail

picks up his board and hits it against a refrigerator, and while it's still in his hands, the board bounces off the refrigerator and adds insult to injury by hitting the kid in the face. It's classic physical comedy. Missing the trick is inconsequential, but the reaction afterward is priceless.

On the positive side, there's *Jason McElwain Autistic Basketball Player* (2.8 million views). McElwain, a high-functioning autistic teenager, was manager of his high school basketball

Jason
McElwain

team. In the last few minutes of the last home game of the season, the coach put him in to play for the first time. After missing a few shots, McElwain hit a three-pointer—and the crowd went wild. And then McElwain hit another three-pointer.... And another.... By the end of the game, he had played for four minutes and scored 20 points. It's an amazing story.

What makes this video so contagious is that it simply shows us the emotional moments, the reactions to his performance. The storytelling is just the absolute minimum setup that we need to understand the payoff: McElwain's hitting those baskets and the crowd's reaction. When the fans in the video jump to their feet, our emotions surge with them. Every time. When everyone rushes onto the court at the end of the game, it's hard *not* to get caught up in their elation. That surge of excitement and happiness motivates sharing.

When you show us something unforgettable in your online video, don't just show us the skill or unforgettable moment itself. Show us the human reactions to that moment too, especially the reactions of the people who just created it. If you show us an amazing leap from rooftop to rooftop, make sure to include the leaper's fist pump of triumph afterward. If you show us a skateboarder wiping out, also show us his disappointment and pain. We crave those human moments of emotion.

We're not talking staged, fake emotion or over-the-top, maudlin tears, but simple, true human feeling. It can be subtle, or it can be broad, but it has to be real.

The Thrill of Victory

What if your video isn't about a basketball player, a skateboarder, or some other athlete? The same rule applies.

When we made *The Extreme Diet Coke & Mentos Experiments*, we had spent months developing dozens of different fountain effects. We had swinging fountains, crossing fountains, spinning fountains, and entire lines of a dozen identical fountains spraying in beautiful synchrony, but we knew that we also had to include at least one moment of real, human emotion. So we used what we call in the circus a *success gesture*, a simple physical movement that would, at the end, physically express how we felt about what we'd just done.

The success gesture is a classic tool from the circus performer and physical comedian's toolbox, and it is a technique we learned about while studying clowning and eccentric performing with Avner Eisenberg at Celebration Barn Theater in South Paris, Maine. Seasoned performers know that often the laugh doesn't come from the pratfall itself but from the performer's reaction in response. When we see a clown slip on a banana peel, we're surprised and maybe a little worried, but when he sits up unhurt, acts as if he fully expected to wind up on the floor, and tries to recover his dignity by cockily adjusting the knot in his tie, we chuckle.

In life, when humans have an emotional moment of success, we instinctively physicalize it with our bodies. We give a thumbs up, we nod our heads "yes," we pump our fists, or, most primal of all, we throw both our arms up in the air in victory. It's in *that* moment, when our humanity is most on display, that anyone watching will connect with us emotionally.

When we were preparing to shoot *The Extreme Diet Coke & Mentos Experiments*, we knew we needed some kind of success gesture at the end. We could have pumped our fists, underplayed it by fastidiously adjusting our ties, or done any of the dozens of hip-wiggling end zone dances football players do after they score a touchdown. Any of those would have worked. What we chose was to throw both arms up in the air in victory. That gesture expressed what we truly felt in that moment of triumph.

Despite the fact that we had invested months of work in developing dozens of Coke and Mentos geyser effects and had painstakingly worked out all that 101-bottle fountain choreography, to this day people consistently tell us that their favorite moment in the video isn't any of that—it's that moment at the end when we throw our arms up in the air in victory.

Why is that?

It's because people respond to emotion in a way that they don't respond to skill alone, no matter how great the skill. When we throw our arms up at the end in triumph, the emotion we are expressing is itself contagious. When you see us expressing our joy, you actually feel a little bit of what we feel.

Researchers like John Cacioppo at the University of Chicago and Elaine Hatfield and Richard Rapson at the University of Hawaii have found that, moment to moment, emotions spread from one person to another, regardless of whether or not we know the underlying reason for the emotions. All we need is to see an emotion being expressed physically, and we start to feel it. We are actually infected with each other's emotions merely by observing facial expressions, posture, and other emotional cues. We are likely to feel sad even if we only see someone crying. We are likely to smile when we simply see someone else smile. This means that success gestures in your videos don't just express your *own* happiness; seeing them also makes *us* feel happy. And to get us in a sharing mood, you want to make us happy.

In creating your own videos, look for your moments of triumph and celebrate them. If you're showing us something you think is great, don't manufacture a reaction; just let us see how it really makes you feel. Show us you like it with even just a smile. If you keep it real, we will feel the emotion that we see you expressing. Infect your audience with positive emotion. Don't overplay your hand, but find the success gestures, however big or small, that will help give your unforgettable content an unforgettable, emotional moment.

The Agony of Defeat

The flip side of the thrill of victory can also be powerful. Not surprisingly, the viral structure for "the agony of defeat" is exactly the same: show us the event, then show us the real, human emotional reaction to it. But remember, to be most contagious, the goal is positive emotion. If we're horrified or think someone has been seriously injured, we're less likely to share than if we're smiling.

From 1970 through the end of *Wide World of Sports'* run in 1998, the images ABC ran in the opening montage over Jim MacKay's words "and the agony of defeat" was footage of Yugoslavian ski jumper Vinko Bagataj hurtling down a ski jump only to fall dramatically just before takeoff. The footage of the awkwardly tumbling Bagataj flying off the ramp, out of control at high speed, looks as though he is surely headed to a gruesome death. Miraculously, however, Bagataj suffered only a concussion and some minor bruises from the fall.

Wide World of Sports Introduction

The footage of Bagataj's ski jumping accident is unforgettable, and in the memories of almost everyone who ever saw the opening of *Wide World of Sports*, it stuck for the rest of their lives. In 1981, when ABC celebrated the twentieth anniversary of *Wide World of Sports*, the network flew a then retired Vinko Bagataj in from Yugoslavia for the celebration. World-class athletes of all stripes who had been featured over the years on the program were in attendance. Yet over the course of the gala, only two received standing ovations: the 1980 U.S. "Miracle on Ice" hockey team and "the agony of defeat guy," Vinko Bagataj.

Seeing the agony of defeat can make for a powerful connection. We can all identify with it. We see it and we know, "There, but for the grace of God, go I." Even the great Muhammad Ali was moved by watching the footage of Bagataj's epic tumble. At the *Wide World of Sports* celebration, Ali himself was one of the first in the crowd that flocked to Bagataj for an autograph.

To go viral with "the agony of defeat" approach takes care. The clip of Bagataj's amazing fall, while unforgettable, is also scary, and videos that frighten us are less likely to be shared than clips that make us happy.

You can do both however. You can show the failure and at the same time make us happy. Vinko Bagataj's ski jump catastrophe, for example, is unforgettable and scary, but the fact that he lived to tell about it is inspiring.

Among the experts at this approach are the folks at *FAIL Blog*. Their bread and butter is people hurting themselves. Sometimes they get you laughing, sometimes they just make you cringe. It's a fine line. If you just make us cringe, that'll be less contagious than if you can make us laugh.

We will admit that *Frustrated Skateboarder Fail* (4.3 million views) makes us laugh, and we can imagine sharing it. It helps a lot

Roman
Candle
Headshot

that at the end the kid doesn't seem badly hurt. On the other hand, *FAIL Blog: Roman Candle Headshot FAIL* (560,000 views), which shows two kids holding lit fireworks and shooting balls of sparks at each other, is over the line for us. The video ends with a ball of sparks shooting right into one kid's face. *Roman Candle Headshot* doesn't make us laugh, and we can't imagine sharing it. Over half a million people watched it, however, so clearly a fair number of people shared it, but concern for how badly the kid may have been hurt is enough to dampen contagiousness.

At its best, *FAIL Blog* finds moments when the agony of defeat is comical and at least safe. Or nearly safe. For example, *Scooter Handling FAIL* (2.8 million views) shows a guy losing control of a scooter and falling down a low embankment. The way he loses control is funny, and most of all, while he really takes a tumble, the driver seems fine and everyone on the scene is laughing. That makes us laugh, and that makes us more likely to share it.

Scooter
Handling
FAIL

One of the classic agony-of-defeat viral videos is *Grape Lady Falls!* (12 million views), which shows Melissa Sander, an Atlanta TV news reporter, falling out of a vat of grapes onto the ground on live TV. As she falls, the camera quickly moves away from her, but off screen we can still hear her howling "Owww, oooh, owww...." The fall doesn't look too bad, and the sounds she makes are peculiar, funny, and seem over-the-top. That combination was enough to get a lot of people laughing and sharing online.

Grape
Lady
Falls!

In fact, what most viewers don't know is that Sander was seriously injured by her fall. She broke a couple of ribs and had to spend two weeks in the hospital recovering. Knowing that makes the video far less funny, and had that information been in the piece, the video would surely have been less contagious. But few people are aware of what actually happened, so *Grape Lady Falls!* is still quite contagious.

If you're looking to explore the agony of defeat, play this game carefully. You can use it effectively, but there are very few videos involving serious injury that go viral.

Again, it's important to recognize that it's not just about the moment when the guy falls on his face or when the girl goes tumbling down the stairs. *Grape Lady Falls!* would have gone nowhere without Sander's off-camera "Owww, oooh, owww" reaction. Because emotions are contagious and because creating viral video is about creating an emotional response in your audience, you not only want to give your viewers something unforgettable, but you also want to include the real human reactions that your unforgettable moment elicited.

In creating your own work, remember that while we want to see the fastball going 96 miles per hour that strikes out the last batter, we *also* want to see the pitcher's teammates mob him on the mound. We want to see the winning home run, but we *also* want to see the players stream out of the dugout for the chaotic celebration at home plate. So show us the dramatic moment, but don't leave out the thrill of victory or the agony of defeat.

⊙ *So Why Don't You Just Throw Your Arms Up in the Air and Skip All That Geyser Stuff?*

While it's true that our "arms up" moment at the end of our videos seems to be everyone's favorite, those videos wouldn't have gone viral if all we had included was that one moment. Before we can throw our arms up in victory at the end of a video, we have to have earned it.

To be true, we have to have put in the effort and we have to have at least tried to do something impressive. Throwing our arms up in the air for no apparent reason wouldn't be an authentic human reaction and wouldn't create a connection with our audience. It would be a false, hollow gesture. But when that same gesture—or fist pump, head bob, end zone dance, or any other success gesture—comes after a real success, or even just an earnest effort, it almost always elicits a smile. In fact, this is true even when that effort results in utter failure. Surprisingly, if there's a genuine attempt to succeed, a success gesture will almost always get a smile, regardless of the result.

Our point here isn't to have you thrust your arms up in the air at the end of all of your videos (although we admit that that's exactly what we do). Rather, it's to make sure you include some sort of authentic human reaction to whatever is the core content of your video.

Interestingly, though we didn't know it at the time, it turns out that of all of our possible choices for a success gesture—and any one of them would have worked—we happened to pick what is probably the most powerful, compelling, and emotional gesture of success there is: arms up over the head. Research has shown that humans from cultures all over the world automatically react to victory by standing tall and raising both arms in the air. Indeed, the gesture appears to be hard-wired into us. Studies conducted by psychologists Jessica Tracy and David Matsumoto analyzed participants' physical reactions to winning and losing at the Olympic and Paralympic Games, focusing in particular on comparing the reactions of those competitors who had been blind since birth with those of sighted athletes. The blind athletes and the sighted athletes, from cultures all around the world, reacted identically to victory: standing tall, expanding their chests, and raising both arms high in the air. Since those athletes who were blind from birth could not have learned the gestures from watching others, and they were not likely taught to react to victory in that manner, Tracy and Matsumoto concluded that the arms-up gesture appears to be a hard-wired response to victory that is coded deep in the human DNA. Apparently, we do it automatically.

CHAPTER 15

Show Humanity, Not Perfection

Numa Numa

On December 6, 2004, 18-year-old Gary Brolsma recorded a 99-second video of himself sitting in his room in front of his computer, lip-synching and mugging to the obscure Eastern European pop song "Dragostea din Tei" by the Moldovan-Romanian boy band O-Zone.

The result was silly and strange, but oddly compelling. Brolsma then edited the footage to make it even odder, intercutting a collection of random still images such as a photo of cheese where the Romanian lyrics *"fericirea"* (happiness) sounded to Brolsma roughly like "feta cheese." He then posted his lip-synch and random-image mashup, *Numa Numa Song*, to the early Internet video site Newgrounds.com. The comments Brolsma got from the Newgrounds

Numa Numa

community urged him to remove the random images and upload just the unedited lip-synch footage, which he did. It was that simpler, more compelling footage that caught on most dramatically.

Now Brolsma isn't the dapper guy with styled hair, charming dimples, and glistening teeth who might get cast in a soft drink commercial. He's an ordinary kid with glasses, who Alan Feuer and Jason George of the *New York Times* described, with unnecessary meanness, as "a pudgy guy from Saddle Brook."

But the guy in that video is *real,* and his video is one of the most popular of all time. According to *BBC News, Numa Numa* received an incredible 700 million views in the first year it was online.

Although Feuer and George looked down their noses at Brolsma's video as "an arm-flailing, eyebrow-cocked performance" that "could only be described as earnest but painful," the rest of the world loved it, and loved Brolsma. Douglas Wolk, writing in the *Believer,* admired the contagious joy and exuberance in the piece. Wolk recognized early on that the fact that Brolsma was an ordinary guy, not a Hollywood actor type, was part of what made his video so compelling. Wolk wrote:

> *Brolsma's video singlehandedly justifies the existence of webcams. His squarish head and shoulders are in the center of the shot. He's got a short haircut, glasses that are slightly too small for him and reflect his computer's monitor, and cheap headphones; he's sitting in a dismal-looking suburban room. And he is going for it.... It's a movie of someone who is having the time of his life, wants to share his joy with everyone, and doesn't care what anyone else thinks.*

As Wolk noted, it was in large part Brolsma's ordinary guy-ness that made the video so appealing. It's hard to watch *Numa Numa* and not smile because as we watch it, we know what we're seeing is a real person, not an actor sent from central casting.

That real person was so contagious that people were watching Brolsma's video by the millions and passing it on to their friends, and they were also so caught up with it that they began joining in *Numa Numa* madness and making their own homage videos to his surprise hit.

Sure, the video is odd. Brolsma made it that way on purpose because he thought that the music, along with his intentionally oddball lip-synching, was funny. Through all of its strangeness, however, there is an irresistibly infectious sense of fun and play that makes us smile.

While a few like Feuer and George at the *Times* belittled Brolsma as though he didn't know what he was doing, they just didn't get it. Defending Brolsma against the idea that he didn't appear to know how strange his video had made him look, Brolsma's friend Randall Reiman explained to the *Times*, "He's been entertaining us for years so [now] it's kind of like the rest of the world is realizing that Gary can make you smile."

Douglas Wolk contrasted Brolsma in *Numa Numa* with the famous video of the *Star Wars Kid*, whose adolescent imitation of a lightsaber battle made him the subject of relentless online ridicule. Wolk observed perceptively that while "everyone laughed at the *Star Wars Kid*, everyone wanted to be the *Numa Numa* Guy—to feel that un-self-consciously self-conscious joy he felt in his body."

Star Wars
Kid

Here, once again, the path to contagiousness is through authenticity and humanity. Like Gary Brolsma, don't try to be perfect. Show us real people, and embrace the fact that humans aren't perfect. It turns out that we actually respond more strongly to imperfection.

Imperfection Is Contagious

Like Gary Brolsma, the people in the wedding party in *JK Wedding Entrance Dance* are not the best dancers you've ever seen, nor the most glamorous, and that's *better*. Imperfections are important because, like good sideshow, they show us real people to whom we can relate. Your video will have a better chance of going viral if it shows us imperfect, real people rather than shiny, well-lit models.

This same principle is at play in viral hits like Matt Harding's *Where the Hell Is Matt? 2008* and Judson Laipply's *Evolution of Dance*. Laipply's never going to be mistaken for a star of the Bolshoi Ballet, but that's *good*. He's real, and real is what we want. The "dance" that Matt Harding takes around the world in his videos is so plain, so simple, that it's a stretch even to call it a dance, but his work is some of the most compelling short video we've ever seen. Notice that what Harding adds as his video develops and becomes more and more engaging is simply more *real* people of every size, shape, and nationality, dancing in whatever quirky, fun, playful, awkward way they naturally move, and *that* made real magic which people couldn't help but spread online.

In fact, before he made *Where the Hell Is Matt? 2008*, Harding had made a similar video, *Where the Hell Is Matt? 2006* (18 million views), which also showed clips of him doing his dance in front of famous landmarks around the world. When he was in Rwanda finishing that 2006 video, however, he suddenly realized that the piece he really should have been making was slightly different—something with more humanity. It was then that he had the idea for what would become *Where the Hell Is Matt? 2008*.

When Stephen talked to him about what happened in Rwanda, here's how Harding described it:

I had a friend who was working at an NGO in Rwanda, and I met up with him. I wanted to shoot a dancing clip there, and every-where I went, I just looked for what is the iconic location in this area. And there really isn't one—the iconic location in Rwanda is Hotel Rwanda, which is not something you want to dance in front of. So, really, all there was to dance with in Rwanda was kids, people.

So I did that, and I went to a remote village outside of the capital and went up to a group of kids that was playing, and I couldn't communicate with them. I didn't speak any Rwandan, they didn't speak any English, so I just started dancing. I had the camera rolling, and they just immediately started dancing too—and had so much fun. Within a couple of minutes, the whole village was standing around in a circle watching us all dance together, and I had this really great experience with these kids. Realizing that it transcended language and it connected us, and I'm sounding really corny here, but it was a really profound moment for me, and it made me go back to the hotel that night and go, "I'm an idiot. I've been doing this wrong the whole time! I'm running around trying to find the Taj Mahal, and I should have just been finding kids, and adults, anybody—just people."

People are so much more interesting to look at.... So after I finished that video, it did pretty well, but I felt like I'd been doing it wrong, so I went back to Stride and said, "You guys have to give me a bunch more money and send me around the world again for a year, because I gotta do this all over again."

And they were nice enough—and the video did well enough for them—that they were like, "All right. . . ." So they sent me off, and I was able to take all the e-mails I got from the people that saw the 2006 video that said, "You forgot to come to Sweden," "You forgot to come to South Korea," "You forgot to come to Israel,". . . , and I was able to write to them and say, "Hey, I'm coming to you. Come out and dance with me." And it became less about this dancing guy who gets to travel around the world and more about here are what people all over the world look like doing the same thing.

That said so much more. I finally had found something worth saying with the videos. And I felt really good about how that turned out.

And with good reason. *Where the Hell Is Matt? 2008* is one of our favorite videos of all time. Why? It's nothing but real people. There is no makeup, there are no sets, there is no artifice. It's just moment after moment of unvarnished, happy humanity.

The more deeply steeped in conventional media you are, where artificial movie star glamour is the norm, the harder this approach can be to accept. In an NPR feature about OK Go's first viral hit, *A Million Ways*, host Robert Siegel noted with some surprise that the dancers in the piece were the band members themselves who were decidedly *un*glamorous, even nerdy. As Siegel put it, the stars of the video "look like four guys from the Apple Genius Bar who are filling in for the LA Laker Girls."

That everyday, unpolished look, of course, was one of the secrets to their success. Had OK Go hired the shiny, perfect, pneumatic LA Laker Girls to dance in the video instead of dancing in it themselves, they would never have had the success with it that they did. The LA Laker Girls are good at what they do, but the guys in OK Go are good at being themselves, and that authenticity, that humanity, was important to helping *A Million Ways* go viral.

So when making your own videos, never forget that if you allow your work to show the imperfections of humanity, we will be more likely to relate to it and to share it. As Trish Sie advises, "Don't worry about looking cute or pretty or sexy or handsome. There's no place in this for that." Instead, dance your imperfect heart out the way the wedding party did in *JK Wedding Entrance Dance*. Just wear a T-shirt and jeans the way Judson Laipply does. Show us what makes different people unique the way Matt Harding does. Or just turn your web cam on and be your weird, fun, compelling, likable self, the way Gary Brolsma did.

Free Hugs

Free Hugs
Campaign

One more example of showing your audience humanity instead of perfection shows up in the peculiar subgenre of viral videos that feature people out on the street offering free hugs to passersby. Juan Mann's *Free Hugs Campaign* is the most popular, with 73 million views. But this viral phenomenon seems to trace back to a music video: the Dave Matthews Band's 2001 *Everyday*.

The video for *Everyday*, a.k.a. *The Hug Guy*, features the scruffy, unshaven Judah Friedlander (now known for playing comedy writer Frank Rossitano on NBC's *30 Rock*) walking through downtown Charleston, South Carolina, and Greenwich Village, asking people on the street for hugs. Initially passersby avert their eyes and avoid him, but eventually, he starts to get a few tentative hugs and the end result is surprisingly heartwarming.

Everyday a.k.a. The Hug Guy

Like Gary Brolsma, Judah Friedlander does not come across as the conventional Hollywood choice. With oversized glasses, trucker hats, and long hair, he's cultivated a look that makes him a great, relatable man-on-the-street.

While *The Hug Guy* had a substantial budget and included appearances from celebrities including Conan O'Brien, Sheryl Crow, and the New York Giants running back Tiki Barber, the star—the guy we remember and identify with—is ordinary guy Judah Friedlander. In casting for the video, Friedlander was the perfect choice to be the Hug Guy, much better than, for example, Brad Pitt would have been. Friedlander's unkempt Hug Guy just plain seems more real and *real is what people are yearning for online*. Don't get us wrong: we like pretty people as much as anyone—and we're almost sure that Brad Pitt is real. But let's face it: he's no Judah Friedlander. The surprising lesson is that to go viral, a Judah Friedlander look is often a better choice than a Brad Pitt look.

⏵ So Why Aren't My Home Movies Going Viral? They're Overflowing with Humanity!

Oh, the humanity.

It's easy to think that Rule Four is all you need. It's not sufficient.

You can't forget Rule Three, Be Unforgettable, or Rule Two, Don't Waste My Time. The world is filled with videos of vacations and dance and piano recitals that show humanity in all its imperfect glory. But most of them won't go viral because if you don't know the people, and sometimes even if you do, they're usually rather forgettable and/or agonizingly long. So don't forget that while humanity is ultimately what it is all about, it needs support from the other rules.

CHAPTER 16

FOR MARKETERS:
Let Your Brand Be Human

Will It Blend?

In conventional advertising, you can craft every moment to present your brand perfectly, down to the tiniest details. A chewing gum brand, for example, would typically have requirements so specific that the company would prescribe the exact method actors should use to put the company's gum into their mouths. Every logo shot must be gorgeous. Every brand message must be consistently presented. The goal is to get everything as close to perfect as possible. When you're paying for conventional advertising, you have complete control over the conversation.

In viral video, however, it's not all about you.

You don't just want us to watch your message. You want us to share it with our friends. So make your videos friendly and relatable, not stiff and corporate. Humanizing your brand this way helps create the emotional connection that will lead to sharing.

The metaphor we find useful here is to think of a video as a gift you are giving to your audience. You want your gift to make us smile, so that when we think of you, we smile all over again.

This meshes perfectly with one of the strategies we talked about in Chapter 9, "No #&$@ing Product Shots": be the source of something cool.

Videos like Stride Gum's *Where the Hell Is Matt?* series, Sony Bravia's *Balls*, and the multiple viral hits from T-Mobile and Cadbury, each give us something cool, uplifting, and fun, ending simply with one or two title cards telling us who it's from. These videos are gifts, and the most important brand presence boils down to this: "We hope you enjoy this—T-Mobile."

Like a gift from one person to another, these gifts should also come with no strings attached. Savvy brands put their videos out there and leave it up to us to visit their websites, learn more about them, and continue the conversation. They understand that if they create good feeling and trust, we'll be happy to see them again.

So give us a gift with your video. Don't weigh it down with heavy branding. Make it easy for us to find your website and your products, but don't pressure us. Remember that if we like your gift, we'll like you, and we'll be likely to tell our friends about this cool video we just watched—the video that the cool folks at your brand gave us.

If we feel like you're selling us something, we'll get our guard up, but if you give us something awesome with no strings attached, we will love you for it.

Making It About Your Audience

Good gifts show an understanding of the people they're for, so you need to be sure to give us what we actually want. In product development and marketing, this is "knowing your customer." In viral video, making something contagious is also about knowing your customer. What will make us happy? Giving us that will get us sharing.

The perfect corporate packaging of the perfect corporate message is anything but contagious. Carefully scripted dialogue that nails all your specific campaign messages feels unnatural. Perfect product shots look fake.

Keep it human. Humans have rough edges. We aren't perfectly on-message, we don't go through life with scripts, and we don't always turn your logo toward the camera.

The two of us have been lucky enough to work with a few brands that really get this, to the point that we've sent them rough test footage and they've been prepared to run with it with no extra polishing. That's great. It means they're not focused on whether the shirts we're wearing are just right or whether that product shot could feature the logo a bit more prominently. They're willing to let the video be human, and they're focused on the two things that matter: (1) Does this represent my brand well? and (2) Is this as contagious as possible?

The *Will It Blend?* series nails this, making brilliant use of CEO Tom Dickson's natural personality. He's a bit goofy, and it would have been so easy for Blendtec to have gone instead with a polished, professional spokesperson and a detailed scripting of the Blendtec value propositions.

But Dickson can't be beat. He comes off as a real guy, and we really connect with him and his ongoing mission to blenderize everything under the sun.

In Chapter 9, "No #&$@ing Product Shots," we advised you to keep your brand presence to the absolute essentials. We pointed out that you have a choice between a conventional video with 10 interrupting product shots that may get 20,000 views and a viral video with one integrated product shot that can get 2 million views.

Here, we're suggesting that you keep your brand presence natural and personal. Let it be imperfect so that it can be more contagious. Which would you prefer: a perfect video that delivers 100 percent of your corporate message and gets 20,000 views, or a more human video that focuses on giving the viewer a great feeling about your brand and gets 2 million views?

Making viral video is about your audience, not just about you. Give us what we want to see, not what you want us to see. Let your brand be human, and give us a gift that will be part of a great relationship.

A Story of Redemption

About a week after we put our first Coke and Mentos video online, we had already had millions of views.

Mentos was quick to react with enthusiasm for the growing viral phenomenon, but the *Wall Street Journal* reported a different reaction from Coca-Cola:

> *"It's an entertaining phenomenon," said Coke spokeswoman Susan McDermott. "We would hope people want to drink [Diet Coke] more than try experiments with it." Coke could use some extra buzz right now. Sales volume of Diet Coke in the U.S. was essentially flat last year, as consumers switch from diet sodas to bottled water and other noncarbonated drinks. But Ms. McDermott says that the "craziness with Mentos . . . doesn't fit with the brand personality" of Diet Coke.*

Blogs and the press had a field day with that reaction. The headline on the *Motley Fool* summed it up: "Coke Is an Idiot."

It was an unfortunate misstep, showing a very traditional reaction to something consumers were really enjoying. It made Coca-Cola look out of touch and too stiff to have a good time.

Coca-Cola's digital marketing team, however, was quick to recognize the mistake and the missed opportunity. They went on to sponsor several successful viral videos, including our Diet Coke and Mentos domino effect and our two Coke Zero and Mentos–powered rocket cars. Since that first knee-jerk reaction to the viral phenom-enon, Coca-Cola has shown a lot of wisdom in social media and viral video, finding ways to give their gigantic brand a relatable, human presence.

The company really showed that it had learned from its experi-ence with the geyser phenomenon when a fan-created Coke page appeared on Facebook and Coke fans began "liking" it by the mil-lions. Rather than squashing it as other brands might have done (or as even Coca-Cola might have done in the past), Coca-Cola stayed human. They encouraged the fan page and made it a huge win for everyone.

When you can take just one step away from corporate rigidity and embrace what your customers love like Coca-Cola and Mentos have, they'll love you for it.

Whether your brand makes cool stuff happen the way that Coca-Cola and Mentos do or you give your brand a real human face the way Blendtec does, viral video is a great opportunity to get past the traditional advertising mindset and let your brand be human.

⊙ So How Do We Keep from Looking Too Corporate?

When you've finally created a video that delivers an unforgettable emo-tional moment, don't kill that moment with clumsy corporate messaging.

Be like a friend, not A Friend®, Inc.

We have had many friendly debates with our clients on how best to integrate their brands into videos, and we see part of our job as keeping them from coming across as too corporate. It often comes down to small, simple things, but they really make a difference.

With this in mind, what we've done when working with Coca-Cola and Mentos is to close our videos with a plain title card saying simply:

Thanks to
The Coca-Cola Company
and Mentos
for helping make this possible.

This positions them as our friends. Our human, approachable friends. For online video (and probably everywhere else), that's a much stronger position than looking like an impersonal, corporate behemoth.

One of the many tip-offs that the *Disneyland Musical Marriage Proposal* was a faked corporate production and not a real moment captured on video was its YouTube description, which read:

> *A magical moment happens on Main Street, U.S.A., when a young man proposes to his girlfriend on a Summer evening in Disneyland® Resort.*

Does this sound like a description any normal person would write? How could we fix it?

First, we'd get rid of the team of lawyers and marketing executives who insisted on using the phrase "Disneyland® Resort" instead of what every normal person calls it: Disneyland. (And for Pete's sake, who uses a registered trademark "®" symbol in a YouTube video description?!)

Eliminating that would give us this:

> *A magical moment happens on Main Street, U.S.A., when a young man proposes to his girlfriend on a Summer evening at Disneyland.*

Better. Of course, a normal person would probably just say "Disneyland" instead of "Main Street U.S.A... at Disneyland." We sure would. Which would leave us with this:

> *A magical moment happens at Disneyland when a young man proposes to his girlfriend on a Summer evening.*

The marketer speak is still lurking in "magical moment" and "on a summer evening," and "young man" and "girlfriend" are impersonal.

How would you write this description if you were talking to your friends?

How about this:

> *John's awesome proposal to Erica at Disneyland.*

The video itself still feels like a corporate production, but now the description is much more human.

If it looks like it's from your marketing department, people are likely to skip right over it, and it won't go viral. You may have worked into it all your marketing messages and beautiful logos, but if the result feels corporate and calculated, no one will share it.

Keep it human.

Music

Why is sound the only sensation that excites the feelings?

Even melody without words has feeling.

But this is not the case for color or smell or taste.

—ARISTOTLE, *PROBLEMATA*, BOOK XIX.27

Viral video is about making an emotional connection. Everything in this book is aiming for that positive, active emotional response that gets people clicking on the "share" button.

After all is said and done, after you've found something true, made sure you're not wasting our time, taken what you've got all the way to unforgettable, and showed us moments of humanity, there's one more secret weapon in your arsenal: music.

Music is a direct line to emotion.

Evolutionary psychologist Steven Pinker, writing in his book *How the Mind Works*, observed:

Music appears to be a pure pleasure technology, a cocktail of recreational drugs that we ingest through the ear to stimulate a mass of pleasure circuits at once.

And in *This Is Your Brain on Music*, cognitive psychologist and musician Daniel Levitin tells us this:

Far more than language, music taps into primitive brain structures involved with motivation, reward, and emotion.

Researchers are just beginning to understand the mechanisms behind this powerful effect, but there's little question of the impact. In all cultures and age groups, music has a unique power to spark emotion.

Music in a major key tends to make us happy. Music in a minor key tends to make us sad. Music can change our heart rates and galvanic skin responses—it's that primal. Just rhythm and melody alone can make us calm or excited, frustrated or content.

We don't need to worry about how or why here. We just need to recognize that music is a path straight to the emotions, and it is therefore an incredible tool for making something contagious.

You can use music to help amplify our positive emotional reaction to your video. You can use the energy music provides to make us more excited. Music alone can provoke the active, positive emotions that promote sharing. When you combine music with unforgettable visuals and moments of true human emotion, you've got something that will be highly contagious.

Accentuate the Positive

From Sony Bravia's *Balls* and *Where the Hell Is Matt? 2008* to *JK Wedding Entrance Dance* and *Evolution of Dance*, many of the best viral videos of all time heighten their emotional impact through great music.

In *Where the Hell Is Matt? 2008*, would the huge ocean wave that crashes down on him on the coast of Tonga pack the same emotional wallop without the simultaneous crescendo in the music? And where would *JK Wedding Entrance Dance* be without Chris Brown's song "Forever"? It evokes just the right feelings.

For our first Coke and Mentos video, we knew the right music could make a big difference. We tried a lot of different tracks before we found the right one: AudioBody's "You Gotta Tap." And that was time well spent. AudioBody's music was a key part of what made that video a success for us. It pumped up the energy, accentuated the emotional high points, and provided another hook that drew people into the video.

Find the music that will provide the right soundtrack for your video. If you have a great song, that can be more than half the battle. Of all the contagious traits in online video, music is the most readily reproducible.

What a Difference a Song Makes

Parry Gripp's *Baby Monkey (Going Backwards on a Pig)* is a great example of the viral sideshow, but that video isn't the *original* baby-monkey-going-backward-on-a-pig video. That honor belongs to *Monkey Rodeo Movie* from YouTuber akiGOGO. That video has had 680,000 views. Parry Gripp's video—using not just the same concept but the same *footage*—has had 14 million.

What's the difference?

Mostly, it's music.

Baby Monkey

Monkey Rodeo Movie

Monkey Rodeo Movie is two minutes of raw footage with just the natural audio picked up by the camera: people at the zoo talking and laughing, the sounds of other animals in the distance, and the monkey chittering frantically when, at one point, he falls off the pig. akiGOGO includes this explanation in the video's description of how this footage came to be:

> A monkey baby lost his mother and a wild boar baby lost his
> mother are preservated in institution of zoo.
> To encourage lonely monkey baby,
> Zoo staff try many things.
> Mix two babies in same room,

They makes friends, get stayed together every time.
Monkey is a favorite with taking turn in the park, on the
    boar's back.
This is not "Show," but is a scene of walking.

It's a great story and some great footage.

To turn this into a big viral hit, Parry Gripp added a soundtrack.

Parry Gripp is a musician with a knack for remixing Internet videos with catchy (and sometimes, depending on who you are, annoying) soundtracks. His other videos include *Fuzzy Fuzzy Cute Cute* (6.4 million views) which features, yes, fuzzy, cute animals and a catchy, repetitive song, and *Nom Nom Nom Nom Nom Nom Nom* (19 million views), a video of hamsters, rabbits, and other pets chewing to yet another catchy, *very* repetitive song.

For *Baby Monkey*, Parry cut the original video down from almost two minutes to just under one minute, and he added one of his signature, repetitive earworm soundtracks.

That silly song makes the video even more unforgettable. And it boosts two important things: energy and emotion. With music layered on top, the video is more exciting and makes us laugh more. Pumping that active, positive emotion makes it more contagious.

Music vs. Truth

Sometimes, adding a layer of music onto your video can conflict with Rule One, Be True. If you're capturing something true and music wasn't part of what actually happened, then adding music afterward isn't strictly true. For a lot of videos this isn't an issue. When the music is part of what the camera captured, as in *Evolution of Dance* and *JK Wedding Entrance Dance*, and when it's integral to the performance that the video presents, as in videos like ours, OK Go's, or Matt Harding's, there's no conflict. Music is core to the truth of those pieces. But adding music to content that was never intended to have it will make your video less true.

That doesn't necessarily mean you shouldn't do it. Music is such a powerful trigger for emotion that including it can sometimes make a video more contagious even though it also makes the video a little less true.

Strictly speaking, the original *Monkey Rodeo Movie*, with nothing but raw footage, does a better job of staying true than the pumped-up-on-an-earworm *Baby Monkey*, yet *Baby Monkey* is much more contagious. Adding music definitely takes that video up a notch. For other videos, like *David After Dentist*, *Battle at Kruger*, or *The Sneezing Baby Panda*, adding music could be a mistake because it would detract from the power of the raw cinema verité footage.

If your video is like *David After Dentist* where the natural audio is important to the audience's sense of being present at a real event, staying true may be crucial, so leave it alone. No music. Otherwise, see what a song will do. Go for the contagious emotional connection that music provides.

Where to Find Music: A Tough Question

This brings us to an important question that we get asked a lot: "Where do I find music that I can get permission to use?"

Tim Street, of *French Maids TV*, has some recommendations:

> There are royalty-free songs available, that you can use for free on YouTube. You just have to give them a mention in your show notes. There's also royalty-free music that you can buy for $35 or $75. And then you can [also] go on Craigslist and get somebody to score it for free. People that are trying to become composers are always looking for something visual to go with music they've created. So it really boils down to how good of a producer are you and how good are you on Google and Craigslist in finding music.

We've put a list of websites that offer royalty-free music on our site ViralVideoManifesto.com.

Links to
Music
Resources

For us, the best way to find music right now is to find a friendly musician to work with. If you can find an up-and-coming band that is willing to give you permission to use their music, it could work out well for both of you. If you do it right, it's a win-win situation for everyone.

For our videos, we've been fortunate to have worked with our longtime friends at AudioBody from the very beginning. AudioBody's music has been a perfect match for our videos, and our videos have been good for them too: the success of our *Extreme Diet Coke & Mentos Experiments* pushed AudioBody's music to the top of the charts on the independent music website CD Baby.

These days, it's tough to get permission from most major artists to use their music in your videos. It's a problem that we hope the music industry and online video companies like YouTube will solve, by creating mechanisms that allow fair use of songs for fair compensation. When no one is trying to make money, there should be a fair way to allow for use, and when money is involved, there should be a fair way to share it.

Whatever route you choose, however, take the time, and if necessary spend some money, to find the right music for your video. You'll be glad you did.

Start Your Own Epidemic

Be True.

Don't Waste My Time.

Be Unforgettable.

And, Ultimately, It's All About Humanity.

These are our four principles for creating viral video. They're remarkably simple, and they work.

You don't have to hit every rule perfectly, but the more you can stick to all four, the more contagious your viral video will be.

Sure, "Be Unforgettable" is a challenge, but we've tried to point the way for you. The remaining three principles are easy to follow once you let go of the production tricks that have been honed over decades to work so well for television but can kill your video's chances of going viral.

This isn't television. This is the twenty-first-century sideshow.

Be True: We know that it can be tempting to hire writers, actors, and a camera crew and go into a studio or close down a city street so that you can shoot your project where everything's under your control. But if you do, chances are that you'll wind up with something more like Disney's lifeless *Musical Marriage Proposal* than the magic of *JK Wedding Entrance Dance*.

Be guided by the insight Allen Funt had in the 1940s when he was still just another solider in the Army Signal Corps and uncontaminated by the decades of television production techniques that had yet to be discovered: reading from a script can never have the power of real life. That insight gave him a career and a franchise that lasted over half a century, and today it's one of the keys to creating an emotional connection with your audience online.

Don't Waste My Time: Get down to business. Narrative is not your friend. Online, you're in the sideshow business. It's setup and payoff; then get out. Show us your sword swallower. Right away.

Be Unforgettable: Do something different; then *own it.* Explore your corner of the world so thoroughly that you find something no one else has ever seen before. That's what *The Extreme Diet Coke & Mentos Experiments* were all about. That's what OK Go's *Here It Goes Again* and *White Knuckles* are. That's what Matt Harding's *Where the Hell Is Matt? 2008* is. That's what *your* next project can be. Be obsessive about this. You'll find it.

Ultimately, It's All About Humanity: Everything we've said so far is in service of this one. People online today are no different from what they were 30,000 years ago when they were still scratching out an existence on the savanna. People connect with people. The purer the raw, positive human emotion you can provide, the more people will want to share it, and that's what going viral is about. That's why all those laughing baby videos are some of the purest viral content out there.

The Bottom Line Is This: If you want to get your audience to like what you've made so much that they stop what they're doing and share it with their friends, you've got to connect with them in a way that's authentic, human, and unforgettable. And you have to do it quickly.

You've got the tools to do that now. We've spelled out our recipe.

Now that you know what to do, **go do it.**

Go start your own epidemic.

———————

Join us at ViralVideoManifesto.com for a continuing conversation. Share your thoughts, get feedback on your videos, and explore with us how to create contagious videos.

 ViralVideo Manifesto .com

The Four Rules
in Action

[1]

Daft Hands: Harder, Better, Faster, Stronger

What It Is: In June 2007, Carleton College student Austin Hall posted a 3-minute, 45-second video of nothing but his hands. The video opens with a title card with white letters on a black background saying:

Daft Hands
Harder, Better, Faster, Stronger

Daft Hands

The card fades, and we see a blurry, out-of-focus shot of Hall's hands, closed into fists, bobbing slightly to the tune "Harder, Better, Faster, Stronger" by the French techno-pop duo Daft Punk. For nearly a minute, Hall just moves his hands slightly to the music, and nothing much happens. After 51 seconds, the computerized vocals in the song begin with the words:

Work It,
Make It,
Do It,
Makes Us,
Harder,
Better,
Faster,
Stronger.

With each line, Hall extends one or two fingers out of his fists to reveal those lyrics, written on his fingers and on the palms of his hands with black marker. Each finger extends only for the moment that those particular lyrics are sung and then closes back into his fist immediately.

While some fingers have complete words on them, others just have syllables. So to make "harder," for example, he extends his right forefinger to show "hard" written along his finger and "er" written on his palm. And it gets more complicated as the song goes on. He has "nev" written on the back of his left thumb. Putting this next to his right palm makes "nev" "er." Bending his left thumb hides the "n" turning "never" into "ever."

The choreography not only gets more complicated, it also gets *faster.* The lyrics start at about one word or phrase per second, but soon they speed up to several words per second. Hall doesn't miss a thing. With additional words and syllables written on the backs and sides of his hands and fingers, Hall's hands fly through all the lyrics as Daft Punk's computerized voice goes faster and faster:

More Than Hour Our
Never Ever After Work Is Over
Work It Harder Make It Better
Do It Faster Makes Us Stronger
More Than Ever Hour After
Our Work Is Never Over

As the song ends, Hall closes his fists as they were in the beginning, and the video fades to black.

Daft Hands has over 54 million views, and it has spawned an entire genre of videos with lyrics written on body parts, including *Daft Hands: Technologic* (8.2 million views) and *Daft Bodies: Harder, Better, Faster, Stronger* (16 million views).

Links to
These
Examples

How *Daft Hands* Scores on the Four Rules

Be True: *Daft Hands* is a wonderful example of Rule One, Be True. It's shot in a single take with a single static camera. Had there been any edits, we would never have been able to trust that it was shot all in one take and that Austin Hall's performance was really what it appears to be. Even the out-of-focus beginning helps give viewers the feeling that what we're about to see is real and that there are no tricks.

Don't Waste My Time: Once the lyrics kick in, there is no time wasted, and *Daft Hands* builds beautifully, but unfortunately there are 51 long seconds of intro in "Harder, Better, Faster, Stronger" before the lyrics ever begin, and Hall's video wastes our time for almost all of them. He was clearly aware of this. The YouTube description he posted with the video warns, "Wait until… the awesome handjig and be amazed."

Be Unforgettable: This is where Austin Hall really nails it. No one we know had ever seen or heard of this kind of lyric-revealing hand dance before, so the initial hook is good. Then Hall takes that starting point and owns it. He gave a lot of thought to how each of the words or parts of words that he wrote on his hands would work in combination to cover all of the lyrics of the song. Then he rehearsed the physical skills he needed to have mastered to make it all work. *Daft Hands* is another example of how creativity, hard work, and really owning what you're showing us can be all you need to go viral.

Humanity: *Daft Hands* gets good marks here too. First off, the video shows nothing but two human hands. In fact, the premise of the video is that it is taking very inhuman-sounding computerized vocals and music and giving us an organic, human way to see them. Also, Hall didn't pretty things up unnecessarily. He left his wristband on, which helps give us the sense that the hands we're watching belong to a specific, real person. And he wrote the words on his hands by hand with a plain black marker with some irregular thicknesses and smudging. This hand-done printing also adds to the piece's sense of humanity.

Music: The specific music here is (obviously) integral to the piece, and it's perfect. It's got a great beat and a great build from beginning to end.

What We Might Have Done Differently: The only thing we would have done differently for this great piece would have been to work out some hand choreography with Hall's closed fists to give the viewer something to watch during those first slow 51 seconds before the lyrics kick in. A couple of hours working to create something more interesting for that part of the video would have made a major improvement. Alternatively, the video could begin, say, 40 seconds into the song, to give us just a little bit of setup before the payoff. Either way, we would punch up the beginning, but once the lyrics start, we wouldn't change a thing.

[2]

A Dramatic Surprise on a Quiet Square

What It Is: In April 2012, when the cable TV channel TNT was launching in Belgium, it released a video online entitled *A Dramatic Surprise on a Quiet Square*. The video begins with dramatic, almost operatic, orchestral music and a series of title cards saying:

Somewhere in a little town in Belgium
On a square where nothing really
*   happens*
We placed a button

A Dramatic
Surprise
on a Quiet
Square

We see a bright red button on a pedestal in the middle of the square and a big arrow hanging from wires 10 feet above, pointing down at the button. On the arrow is printed, "PUSH TO ADD DRAMA." Then there's one more title card:

And waited for someone to push it

We then see a man on a bicycle slowly riding by, looking the button up and down, looking around the square, and clearly wondering what the consequences will be if he presses the button. We see shots of other passersby skeptically looking at the button. Finally, the man on the bicycle rides up to the button, with his curiosity winning over his trepidation, and he presses it.

A siren goes off. The man on the bicycle jumps at the sound. The video cuts to another shot of a young woman having just pressed the button at another time also jumping at the sound of the siren.

An ambulance pulls up and medics bring a man on a stretcher out from a building, but as they approach the ambulance, they lose their grip, drop the stretcher, and their patient falls hard onto the pavement. We see more and more reactions from people in the square, both bystanders and button-pushers. Then the ambulance starts to pull away before the rear doors are closed, and the stretcher falls out of the back onto the pavement with the patient still on it.

And that's just the beginning of an amazing, escalating series of wild stunts. A bicyclist crashes into the ambulance door. He starts a punching, kicking, whirling fight with the ambulance driver. A girl wearing nothing but red lingerie and a helmet randomly rides by on a motorcycle. An SUV and a police van roar in. Several men with guns pour out of the vehicles, and there's a violent shootout. After one of the gunmen falls to the pavement with blood on his shirt, the rest of the men jump into their vehicles and burn rubber as they race away.

Finally, a group of four American-style football players in full gear runs out of one of the buildings, picks up the fallen gunman, and hustles him back into the building. The woman on the motorcycle drives by one last time, and a two-story sign unfurls down the side of the building:

YOUR DAILY DOSE
OF DRAMA

from 10/04 on Telenet
TNT
WE KNOW DRAMA

All through, we see the reactions of everyday people in the square, particularly those who pushed the button: the first man on the bicycle, the young woman, a teenager, a couple, and more. We see them stare in incredulity at the woman on the motorcycle. We see them flinch and cover their ears when the "gunfire" breaks out. And most important, we see them smile and laugh at the end, with expressions of, "What the heck was that?!" and "Wow!"

The final title cards on the video remind us again of the sponsor of the video:

TNT
WE KNOW DRAMA

How *A Dramatic Surprise* Scores on the Four Rules

This video has gotten over 36 million views—almost three times the total population of Belgium. It turned into a worldwide viral phenomenon that brought big visibility to TNT far beyond its intended audience. For good reason. *A Dramatic Surprise* does an excellent job on the four rules.

Be True: This is classic *Candid Camera*, and within that frame, it does a good job of staying true. While there are many camera angles and edits, they stay true to documenting what truly happened. The cameras are hidden in particular spots, so we don't see unlimited angles; we see the same angles again and again, which reinforces that this is real and it was captured with only a few hidden cameras. The edits blend several occurrences of pushing the button into one sequence, so we experience many people's reactions while just seeing the events once. Those edits save us time, giving us lots of reactions without undermining our sense that this is really happening. Again, this is modern *Candid Camera*: creating wild circumstances and documenting true reactions of real people.

Don't Waste My Time: The video is wonderfully efficient. The title cards at the beginning keep the narrative to a minimum. We don't need any more background on who is doing this or why. The opening titles provide the minimal setup: we need to know this was orchestrated; then we're ready for the *Candid Camera* adventure.

TNT chose to use titles instead of showing the cast and crew getting ready or the hidden cameras being put into position, which would have been more visual (think of the guy loading the Coke machine in *Happiness Machine* that served a similar setup purpose). But here, the title cards serve to set it up efficiently and build the tension nicely.

Be Unforgettable: *A Dramatic Surprise* nails it once again, with an idea that is both different and taken to the extreme. The producers don't just give you one unexpected moment. They *own it*: slapstick, fights, speeding cars, gunfights, even football players and a girl on a motorcycle. They took their idea all the way.

Humanity: Ultimately, this video is all about the reaction shots. We see ourselves and our own reactions reflected in these shots. And the video makers found a great cross-section of people, with different ages and body types—regular folks whom we can relate to. They injected their crazy stunt with a good dose of humanity.

Music: Finally, the music, which continues throughout, definitely infuses the video with drama and energy akin to a movie trailer soundtrack's effect on an audience. It's epic, which suits the absurd spectacle. And the video finishes with silence, allowing the last couple of reaction shots to stand on their own nicely.

What We Might Have Done Differently: Our only suggestion is a very small one: the final shot of the TNT sign unfurling is held longer than necessary. Using our metaphor that a sponsored viral video is a gift from the sponsor, TNT is saying: We gave you this. Remember, we gave you this. Who gave you this? We did. It gets a little redundant. But that is a minor detail in an extraordinary video that really nails building a branded video for extreme contagiousness.

[3]

—

The Little Girl Giant

What It Is: In 2005 and 2006, the innovative French theater company Royal de Luxe brought a remarkable puppet show to London, Antwerp, and Nantes. The show told the story of a time-traveling little girl and an elephant. The remarkable part: the puppet of the little girl was 16 feet tall. The elephant was 40 feet tall. Those are big puppets.

The Little Girl Giant

There are several online videos of these and other Royal de Luxe shows. The most popular we have found is *The Little Girl Giant*, a five-minute video with 3.1 million views.

It begins with a title card:

*The little girl giant
woke up one morning,
got a shower from
the Sultan's Elephant,*

and wandered off to
play in the park...

The music starts, and we see the enormous marionette of the little girl lying down in a pink nightdress, surrounded by people clad in bright red coats, dressed as footmen. The footmen pull on ropes that raise her up. Her eyes open, and she stands, supported from above by ropes hanging from a crane. The footmen move squares of carpet onto the ground in front of her as she walks forward to the elephant.

We see only the tip of the elephant's trunk, as it sprays water down onto the giant girl. The puppeteers move her hands to touch her hair as the water flows down over her. The camera pulls back, and we get one more glimpse of the elephant, this time just its head.

With an edit, the video jumps forward in time to show the girl, now clad in a green dress, having her shoes and socks put on by the footmen. She walks forward, with the crane moving to support her. Her mouth opens, and she sticks her tongue out to lick a giant Popsicle. About two minutes into the video, she walks through a crowd of people and does what appear to be some slow calisthenics.

At the three-minute mark, some real little girls climb up onto her arms to sit while the little girl giant rocks them back and forth. After they climb off, the giant girl then slowly walks to a big chair, sits down, lies back, and goes to sleep. The music fades, and the video fades to black, with a final title card listing the credits for the video.

How *The Little Girl Giant* Scores on the Four Rules

Of all the videos of Royal de Luxe's spectacular puppets, this is definitely one of the best, but a more contagious video could be made.

Be True: *The Little Girl Giant* clearly documents a particular performance, and most of the edits do simply move us forward in time, compressing a show that must have taken quite a long time into five minutes. But many of the edits change perspective without letting us simply observe. Many of the shots are only two to three seconds long, jarring us by activating our orienting response rather than immersing us in the beautiful images. Because of the need to compress a long performance into a short video, one uninterrupted shot of this performance was not an option. However, fewer edits and longer shots would improve the feeling of "I am the camera. Take me there."

There is also one frustrating omission: we don't see the entire elephant. There is a 40-foot-tall elephant puppet standing right there, but we never get more than a partial glimpse of it. To see the whole thing, you have to watch a different video, such as *The Sultan's Elephant* (390,000 views).

The Sultan's
Elephant

Don't Waste My Time: This video does an admirable job compressing the performance down to five minutes. It also minimizes the story, focusing on the spectacle, but it could have gone further in this direction. It seems to have been edited down to the length of the song (the song and the video end at the same time), which is often a sign that a video could be shorter. Here, though the video is five minutes long, the image of the giant girl remains compelling for only about three or four minutes. Remove the requirement to fit the video to the entire song and, without sacrificing clarity, the video could easily be a full minute or two shorter—and consequently more contagious. It's important to remember to be *ruthless* in editing a video to be as short as possible. Even with a money shot, you can give it screen time only as long as it's interesting. The classic movie money shot—a car crash or explosion—can sustain our attention for only so long before we lose interest even in that.

Be Unforgettable: The folks at Royal de Luxe have created something truly unforgettable, and this video captures that. These puppets are enormous and beautiful. The puppeteers dressed as footmen add to the imagery. There are surprises like her tongue being able to lick the Popsicle and the little girls climbing up onto her arms. This rule is where the video excels: its subject matter is astounding.

Humanity: The giant puppet herself exhibits moments of beautiful humanity: when she puts her hand to her hair as the elephant sprays her with water, when she closes her eyes to sleep. The strongest moment of humanity, which could have been captured better and accentuated more, is the girls climbing up onto her arms. Unfortunately the camera is not close enough to see the girls' faces and their smiles as they look up at this 16-foot-tall version of themselves. Those reactions would have been pure gold and would have knocked it out of the park on humanity.

Music: The music, "Decollage," by Les Balayeurs du Désert, was well chosen, and it set the right tone. But it also, presumably, dictated the length of the video when it would have benefited from being shorter.

What We Might Have Done Differently: This video would benefit from being a minute or two shorter with both fewer edits and longer, more continuous shots. Getting closer to the action to see the faces of the girls climbing onto the puppet would have put the icing on the cake. And for crying out loud, let us see the elephant! For all the strengths of this video, we hope that someone will make a video of Royal de Luxe in action that is as unforgettable as their puppets.

[4]

Dude Transports 22 Bricks on His Head

What It Is: Shot in Khulna, Bangladesh, this short video shows two men standing in a large boat filled with bricks. The man on the right balances 2 large bricks, roughly 12 by 6 by 2 inches each, on his head. The other man then hands him 2 more bricks, which he places on top of the bricks already on his head. He then gets 2 more bricks, then 2 more. The man on the left continues to hand over pairs of bricks, and the man on the right continues to take them and place them on top of the others until there are 12 large bricks balanced on his head and the stack is so tall that his arms can no longer reach high enough to place any more on top.

Then without pausing for even a second, the man takes another 2 bricks and gently *tosses* them up on top of the stack already balanced on his head. He then takes 2 more bricks and tosses them up again,

22 Bricks

catching them on top of the previous pair. Then 2 more and 2 more and 2 more, until he is balancing 22 bricks on his head and the stack is nearly as tall as the man himself. Finally he turns, and balancing the entire load on his head, he walks to the end of the boat onto a narrow plank about 20 feet long and no more than 10 to 12 inches wide that provides a makeshift bridge to the dock, and he walks rapidly across it as it sags and bounces slightly under his weight. As the video ends, the next worker steps up to take his load of bricks.

This video has 1.9 million views.

How *22 Bricks* Scores on the Four Rules

Be True: Just from looking at the thumbnail before the video even begins to play, we can tell that this video is true. The video is grainy, and the features of the men in it are hard to discern. It's a gray, overcast day. The workers are wearing mismatched shorts and T-shirts, and the supply of bricks on the boat that is to be unloaded appears to have been dumped in a large disorganized pile rather than stacked neatly. As the video begins, we hear background sounds: the quiet whirring of a small motor and occasional faint voices off camera speaking a language that is not English. As the man begins to stack the bricks, we hear a distinctive ceramic clink as they land on the top of the stack. Though the worker balances the bricks skillfully on his head, his stack is real, not perfectly neat. At one point one of the bricks doesn't land right and falls to the ground as the man casually but quickly steps aside to avoid having it smash onto his bare foot.

The footage was shot with a fixed camera, and the entire video is a single unedited shot. As the man prepares to toss up the twenty-first and twenty-second bricks to the stack, an off-camera voice exclaims quietly in English, "No way!" which is exactly what we were thinking. From start to finish there's never a question as to whether what we're watching is true.

Don't Waste My Time: The entire video is only 44 seconds long. When it starts, the man is already on the boat and has two bricks balanced on his head, and he begins adding bricks to the stack almost immediately. There is no narrative and no mood setting. There are no establishing shots and no moments of unnecessary character introduction. The video ends as the man balancing the bricks walks across the narrow, unsteady plank bridge to the dock and out of frame. Not a moment is wasted. It's all one 44-second money shot.

Be Unforgettable: We've seen a lot of circus acts, and even to us this stunt is a good one. It may be that in Bangladesh, this method of carrying bricks is commonplace, but it's something we'd never seen before, and the image of the stack getting higher and higher as the man tosses up yet another two bricks sticks in our memory.

Humanity: This video is expressly about people. The workers here are real and easy to identify with. The matter-of-fact way in which they go about their rather remarkable business shows both the superhuman and the human. The amazing feats of balance these workers apparently perform every day are inspiring, and the video helps us feel a human connection with them and the lives they lead on the other side of the globe.

The only thing missing is a moment of victory or celebration, but in part, the message of the video is that this circus-worthy balancing stunt is something that these men do every day, so a celebratory moment from them wouldn't be true. The fact that the person shooting the video (or someone nearby) blurts out, "No way!" as the final two bricks are tossed up is the perfect human reaction to what's just happened. That exclamation is from the perspective of someone who, like us, doesn't see this every day, and it helps us more fully appreciate what we've just seen.

Music: This video has no music, and that works very well. The live audio is terrific, and music would generally interfere with the great rawness of the footage. But we could also imagine, for better or worse, Parry Gripp (*Baby Monkey*) giving it an over-the-top infectious soundtrack that would also be effective.

What We Might Have Done Differently: As a single, unedited, candid shot of a remarkable stunt, this video nails it. A simple title card or subtitle in the beginning could help explain a little bit more about what we're seeing—who we're watching and where they are—but that is only a minor issue.

The biggest weakness of this video is something that can't really be changed without undermining one of its strengths: it's not emotional. This is everyday life for these brick carriers, and their matter-of-factness is remarkable and real. While a video of a more emotional moment—say, a competition between brick carriers ending with one victorious and the other standing over a pile of fallen bricks—could be a great video with more contagious emotion, it would also have lost something important: the truth that, for these brick carriers, this is everyday life. But if you could find a way to capture them both, the truth and the emotion, you would have something even more contagious.

[5]

The T-Mobile Welcome Back

What It Is: Following the huge success of *The T-Mobile Dance*, the company's train station flash mob that we discussed in Chapter 9, T-Mobile released *The T-Mobile Welcome Back*. Like the dance video, this video starts with a simple title card showing the location and date of the stunt:

The T-Mobile Welcome Back

The T-Mobile Dance

Heathrow Terminal 5
27th October 2010
No instruments were used in this film.

And like the dance, this is guerrilla theater: an unexpected performance in an unusual location. But this time, the performance is an a cappella medley of songs welcoming people home at the airport.

The video first shows a wide shot of the crowd waiting at international arrivals, and then it cuts to a couple embracing. In a series of quick cuts, we see a woman approach the couple with a flower, starting to sing "At Last," another woman joins in with a vocal "violin" line, the couple is offered the flower (shown from three different camera angles), a man adds in with a vocal percussion line, and three women add in as well, before the song changes. This takes us to the 36-second mark.

With the change in song comes a change in singers. New performers run in and sing to a group of flight attendants. Yet another group sings to a young man as he walks through the terminal. The energy kicks up at 1:30 with a larger group singing with arms outstretched, and the smiles really start spreading in the crowd watching. More groups of singers run up to people walking into the terminal. At 2:00, a man with a beard stands with a stunned expression on his face as a group of singers surrounds him.

At 2:15, the video hits its stride with "I Knew You Were Waiting (For Me)." The lead singer approaches a man waiting with a sign. When he smiles and laughs, we see and hear her smile and laugh in response. That takes us into a final montage to Peters and Lee's "Welcome Home," featuring a series of shots of embraces, high fives, singers with their hands in the air, smiling faces, and a final shot of a girl wiping tears from her face as her friend embraces her and the singers sing behind them.

How *The T-Mobile Welcome Back* Scores on the Four Rules

This video was not as successful as its predecessor (12 million views versus 35 million views), and while *Welcome Back* has its strengths, there are clear places where it falls down on the four rules.

Be True: Like its predecessor, *Welcome Back* captures an elaborately planned, true event, but *Welcome Back* involves the heavy use of production techniques that interfere with that truth. In the first 30 seconds of singing, there are 12 different shots. In the same period of time, *The T-Mobile Dance* has only 4. Overall, *Dance* has a total of 32 shots (still a lot for viral video) while *Welcome Back* has a staggering 82. *Welcome Back* comes at you with an edit every 2.25 seconds. That overstimulates our orienting response and cuts down on contagiousness.

There aren't just too many edits; there are also too many camera angles. *Dance* feels like there were just a few hidden cameras, whereas *Welcome Back* feels like a big-budget professional shoot with cameras everywhere. *Welcome Back* is close to the glossy, perfect-audio, lots-of-cameras feel of *Disneyland Musical Marriage Proposal*, which makes it feel less true.

Don't Waste My Time: *Welcome Back* does well on this. One could quibble on whether or not any trimming could be done—perhaps one or two songs could go—but overall, it keeps things moving.

Be Unforgettable: Again, good marks here. These are interesting, creative situations, and they create compelling reactions.

Humanity: The second big problem is here. Just as *Dance* did a better job of staying true with its production techniques, it also showed us more joyful human reactions. Several of the reactions in *Welcome Back* are awkward because the singers are sometimes aggressive and unintentionally put passersby on the spot. Where the performers in *Dance* just started dancing and people nearby could watch or join in, the singers in *Welcome Back* run up to people and demand a reaction. Particularly take a look at the fellow at 2:00 who finds himself surrounded, with a singer right in his face. He's not alone in a less than joyful reaction.

Welcome Back is at its best when the singer at 2:15 breaks and laughs with the man whom she is singing to. That's a human crack in the otherwise-too-glossy veneer. He is affected by her, and vice versa. That's a great moment of humanity. If more of *Welcome Back* had captured the humanity and joy that it shows in its final minute, it would have been a more contagious video.

Music: The music here is great, providing energy and emotion. Like the camerawork, however, the audio is perfect, with very little sense that it is being performed live.

What We Might Have Done Differently: Most of all, we would use half as many cameras and half as many shots. This video is too glossy and perfect, so we would rough it up with more live audio and less perfect camerawork. And finally, we would bring out more of the joy that we see at the end. We would back off on the aggressive running at people that provokes awkward reactions and instead, focus on the humanity that emerges in the final shots.

[6]

Lachen in der U-Bahn (Laughing in the Subway)

What It Is: Apparently recorded with a camera phone on a German subway, this video opens with a shot of a moderately crowded subway car. A woman in the foreground is looking at her smartphone and chuckling to herself. As she continues to look at her phone, her chuckle grows into a laugh that she can't suppress. The camera pans to another woman nearby who has noticed the first woman, and she too begins to smile and then chuckle to herself. Then, seeing and hearing the first two, another woman standing near them starts to laugh too. Soon the laughter has spread even further, and several people on the subway car are laughing. At this point, the camera returns to the first two women who laughed, now trying to recover the stoic demeanor that is standard subway car etiquette across the

Lachen in der U-Bahn

world, but they have started something contagious, and they can't help but redouble their laughter.

By now, we can hear several people on the train laughing off camera, and we can see down the subway car that people all through the train are starting to smile, grin, and finally chuckle to themselves. Eventually, nearly half the train car is laughing out loud, while at the same time looking a bit perplexed as to what they're laughing at—which of course makes them laugh more. As we watch, we don't know if the first few people knew each other or if they knew what the first woman was initially laughing at, but it's soon clear that complete strangers, far down the subway car, are also laughing out loud. At its peak, the car is filled for a few moments with truly raucous laughter. As the train pulls into the next stop, the laughter subsides a bit, and the video ends.

How *Lachen in der U-Bahn* Scores on the Four Rules

Be True: This cinema verité piece comes across as very real. It's shot with a handheld cell phone camera. It's a single, uninterrupted shot, taken in a real-world location, and it catches real people in an unusually fun moment in their everyday lives.

But the one question that quietly nags at us as we watch this video is, "Is this really spontaneous, or was it planned?" There are slight suspicions raised. How did it happen that this was so well captured on video? It's a little odd that someone on the train had their camera phone trained on the woman who first started laughing almost immediately after she began to laugh. How did that happen? Was it recorded perhaps by the person who had just sent the first woman a text or whatever it was that started her laughing? We don't know. It's odd to find a subway car full of laughing strangers, and even odder that the event was so well recorded from the start.

When we wonder, even just a little, if what we're seeing is real, that hurts the contagiousness of the video. But as the laughter spreads through the train car and it's clear that these people are laughing for real, we begin to enjoy what we're seeing and smile and laugh ourselves even though we have a little doubt as to how it all began.

It turns out that the suspicions we had while we watched were well founded. The laughter that infected this subway car wasn't accidental. It was a laughter flash mob conducted by the *Lachclub Berlin-Mitte*—the Laughter Club of Central Berlin, a group of laughter enthusiasts who regularly get together to practice what's become known as "laughter yoga." Laughter yoga practitioners typically gather together regularly, and after some initial warm-up exercises that might include stretching, clapping, or other gentle movement, they stand in a circle facing each other and begin to laugh artificially. They have found that doing this for a very short time almost always triggers real laughter, which in turn triggers more. Sessions of 20 minutes are common, and practitioners believe that it not only spreads happiness but it also has significant health benefits.

On the November day that the *Lachclub Berlin-Mitte* shot this video, their usual meeting place was closed, so they took the opportunity to try the laughter flash mob seen in *Lachen in der U-Bahn*. A number of them boarded the train separately, stood and sat in different places, and let the first woman start them off. They frankly expected that their stunt would be met with indifference, possibly even resentment, but their hope was to make at least one unsuspecting person happy that night. What they got was far more. To their surprise, the subway car they rode was transformed into as they put it a *"rollenden Lachwagon,"* a rolling laughter wagon. They ended up riding the subway for an entire hour, bringing flash mob laughter to Berlin's commuters.

So in fact what we see in the video isn't quite true. The laughter, which is what the piece is all about, is real (though possibly the first woman who triggers it all may be forcing things in the very beginning), but not everyone on the subway car is as unsuspecting as they seem. Some of them are in on the stunt and join in as though they just happened to be there. We can't tell from watching who's in on it and who's not.

Don't Waste My Time: The results are mixed here. The video does well by starting when the action starts and ending at the right time as the laughter has peaked and is beginning to wane. And it has to take the time to earn its escalation of laughter, but at almost three minutes long, it is slow enough to give viewers a chance to click away. To sustain our interest, you need to give us new information constantly. Sometimes, as in 22 *Bricks*, this is simply giving us more of what we've already seen because the mere fact that there is more of it is important. The ninth and tenth bricks, the eleventh and twelfth bricks, each added more information we wanted. We watch intently to see just how high he can build the stack on his head. In *Lachen in der U-Bahn*, however, our interest peaks sometime before the video finishes, so it winds up wasting some of our time.

Be Unforgettable: This video is fun and engaging, and the 3.2 million views it has had prove that it's contagious, but it isn't the most memorable video we've ever seen. It's got a lot going for it, but for us it doesn't take things quite far enough to really cross the threshold into unforgettable territory. It is something we've never seen before, but it doesn't go all the way into owning it.

Humanity: Here, this video is nearly perfect. What could be more universally human than laughter? *Lachen in der U-Bahn* shows us nothing but laughter and how it spreads among us. As we discussed in Chapter 14, "Give Me the Thrill of Victory and the Agony of Defeat," it is human nature to respond emotionally ourselves when we see other people's emotional reactions, even when we haven't experienced whatever it was that originally caused their reactions. As *Lachen in der U-Bahn* shows, we laugh when other people are laughing even when we don't know what they are laughing about. This is pure, positive emotion, which is why it's so contagious—both inside the subway car and when we watch the video of it.

Music: There is none, and none is needed.

What We Might Have Done Differently: There are only two things here we would consider changing. First, there's no need to hide the fact that some of the people on the subway car are in on what's going on. This is *Candid Camera*, so let us know who's part of the laugh mob and who was just lucky enough to be there when it happened. The tinge of distrust we felt watching the opening when we weren't quite sure why the camera happened to be recording the first woman just at the right moment could have been eliminated had there been some brief introduction explaining what was going on. A title card that said something along the lines of "Six members of the Berlin Laughter Club start a mini-laughter epidemic on the subway" would have made the video stronger. Acknowledging that this is a *Candid Camera* situation would put us in on the joke, increase the truth of the video, and create curiosity to see how the situation will play out.

The other thing we'd love to see is more people. Take it all the way to owning it. Would it be possible to infect an even bigger crowd somehow? Could this be done with (or is it *to*?) an entire football stadium full of people? If so, video of that would really be unforgettable.

Time-Lapse Comparison: Skyscrapers, Jigsaw Puzzles, and Noah Kalina

What It Is: Time-lapse videos online range from *Ark Hotel Construction Time Lapse Building 15 Storeys in 2 Days* (5.6 million views) and *Noah Takes a Photo of Himself Every Day for Six Years* (23 million views) to an amazing number of videos showing people putting together jigsaw puzzles (a quick search turns up videos with anywhere from 31 views to 18,000 views).

These videos generally don't involve any surprises. At the beginning, there's an empty table or a hole in the ground. At the end, there's a

Ark Hotel Construction Time Lapse Building 15 Storeys in 2 Days

Noah Takes a Photo of Himself Every Day for Six Years

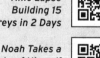

jigsaw puzzle or a skyscraper. And, yes, Noah Kalina took a picture of himself every day for six years. At the end, he looks a little bit older. Not a lot of surprise there either.

Like a lot of home videos, the jigsaw puzzle time-lapses clearly fall down on Rule Three, Be Unforgettable. Without finding a real twist on the idea, these videos are just too mundane to be contagious and to rise above a few thousand views. A skyscraper going up in two days and a guy taking over 2,000 photos of himself—each of those has enough of a hook to be contagious. Let's compare these two videos.

Ark Hotel Construction

This is the more popular of two successful time-lapse videos of skyscrapers going up from YouTube user differentenergy. *Ark Hotel Construction* begins with a title card in Chinese and a graphic of the Earth as seen from space that zooms in repeatedly to show the location in China where this building is being constructed. From 0:15 to 0:42, we see a montage of construction images, some in time-lapse, of cranes moving platforms into place, workers installing beams and panels, and people wearing hardhats pointing and speaking into megaphones.

At 0:42, the pure time-lapse begins. This is a single, wide, fixed-camera shot that shows the entire construction site, with an on-screen counter in the lower left showing the elapsed time. Six giant cranes move a steady stream of building components off of arriving trucks, and the structure gets taller and taller. In 48 seconds, we see almost 48 hours' worth of nonstop construction fly by, ending with the completed 15-story skeleton of the building. After a pause of a couple seconds, the time-lapse continues, now showing the skin going on the skeleton. After 20 more seconds of video that compress 86 more hours of finishing work, the building is complete. The video ends with five quick aerial and time-lapse shots showing the final results. Altogether, the video is 2 minutes and 12 seconds long.

Noah Takes a Photo of Himself Every Day for Six Years

Photographer Noah Kalina's time-lapse self-portrait begins with a single title card:

everyday

For the next five minutes, with a minimalist piano score in the background, we see six years go by in a progression of photos of Kalina's face. His hair sometimes changes, and his surroundings may vary, but always, his face is there in the center of the screen, almost emotionless and almost unchanging. At the end, the "everyday" title card reappears, followed by:

January 11, 2000 – July 31, 2006
2356 days
a work in progress
by Noah Kalina

The video ends with 20 more seconds of title cards, such as "original music by Carly Comando" and "copyright 2006 all rights reserved."

How *Ark Hotel Construction* and *Noah Takes a Photo of Himself Every Day for Six Years* Score on the Four Rules

Be True: Both videos stay true, but *Noah Takes a Photo* is shot in true and contagious style. It has classic, simple, low-production values: just a guy and a camera. In contrast, the first 42 seconds of *Ark Hotel Construction* are computer graphics and an assortment of high-production shots. *Ark Hotel Construction* doesn't get to "Just press record and do it" until the core time-lapse shot. There, it nails it. Many other construction time-lapse videos are so wide and messy that it's hard to see what's happening. *Ark Hotel Construction* does a great job in its primary shot of showing us what's happening and what it would be like to be there.

Don't Waste My Time: Once again, those first 42 seconds of *Ark Hotel Construction* are hurting the video's contagiousness. Do we need that zoom-in from space or the guy with a megaphone? We're here to see a skyscraper go up. Show us the money shot.

 Noah Takes a Photo gets right to it, but it has a different, more challenging problem: it's more than twice the length of *Ark Hotel Construction*. Given that there are no surprises, five minutes is a long time to just watch someone's face, but one of the things that makes the video impressive is the sheer volume of photos he took. Taking the time to watch all those images has a powerful, hypnotic effect. It's a trade-off: be shorter so people don't wander off, or be longer and show a more impressive number of images. It's a tough decision. Certainly the long closing credits of *Noah Takes a Photo* are hurting its contagiousness. To go through 46 seconds watching nine one-line title cards wastes our time and sends us on our way at the very moment we could be clicking the "share" button.

Be Unforgettable: Both these videos are unforgettable, but in different ways. We've never seen such a tall building go up so fast, and we've never seen such an extensive, obsessive time-lapse self-portrait. Each has a good hook, but interestingly what makes Noah Kalina's video so unforgettable is that it shows him. It is memorable because it excels at Rule Four, Ultimately, It's All About Humanity.

Humanity: This is where Noah Kalina hit a home run. And it's a repeatable formula. From Ahree Lee's *Me: Girl Takes Pic of Herself Every Day for Three Years* (9 million views) to *Natalie Time Lapse: Birth to 10 Years Old in 1 Minute 25 Seconds* (7.3 million views), a simple search for "photo every day" turns up a dozen videos with over 1 million views, including a spoof, *Ben Takes a Photo of Himself Every Day*, with 2.9 million views. But a simple search for "construction time-lapse" turns up only two videos with more than a million views, both from YouTuber differentenergy. Humanity is more contagious than construction. This rule is *Noah Takes a Photo*'s greatest strength and *Ark Hotel Construction*'s greatest weakness.

Music: The music for *Ark Hotel Construction* is effective and provides energy, but the music for *Noah Takes a Photo* is essential and establishes the poetic, emotional tone for this video.

What We Might Have Done Differently: *Ark Hotel Construction* would benefit from losing most of its first 40 seconds of setup shots, and *Noah Takes a Photo* would benefit from losing almost all of its 40 seconds of closing credits. Other than that, we would add some humanity to *Ark Hotel Construction*, particularly at the end. While some of the setup shots show real people and add humanity, they focus on what the people are doing and have no emotional content. A short, simple group shot of all the construction workers gathered together at the end celebrating their achievement would add greatly to this video. For *Noah Takes a Photo*, we would consider making the core of the video shorter, but it's such a poetic achievement, with far greater emotional impact than any of the similar videos we've seen, that we'd be extremely cautious of tampering with it.

[8]

"Torn," by David Armand and Natalie Imbruglia

What It Is: In 2005, British comedian David Armand appeared on HBO performing a short, silent act in which he rapidly mimed each word or phrase in Natalie Imbruglia's cover of the Ednaswap song "Torn" while the song played over the PA system. A short excerpt of the HBO performance was posted on YouTube under the title *Karaoke for the Deaf.* That copy has 520,000 views, which was a good number in the early days of YouTube. Since then, several different versions and different performances of Armand's act have been posted, and they have gone viral. Here we take a look at two of them, starting with the single-camera, live performance in *Dance Interpretation of "Torn," by David Armand* (posted on February 22, 2006, with 950,000 views).

Dance Interpretation of "Torn," by David Armand

The video starts with a black screen. A voice with a slight British accent comes over the PA system quietly intoning, "Ladies and gentlemen, would you please welcome to the stage Vienna's foremost interpretive dance *artiste*, Mr. Johann Lippowitz [a character name Armand sometimes uses], who tonight will be giving you his interpretation of the songs of Natalie Imbruglia." There's a smattering of applause from the live audience as a single spotlight comes up on a blank stage in front of a closed red curtain. For several seconds we see just the curtain, and then into the spotlight walks David Armand, clad in black slacks, a long sleeve, collarless, button-down, black shirt with the sleeves rolled up above his elbows, and a close fitting black knit cap.

Showing no expression, he carefully adjusts the drape of his shirt, shakes his hands as if to loosen them up, does a few arm stretches, points to the back of the theater to cue his music, and stands, looking straight ahead, with his arms down, hands clasped in front of him. Natalie Imbruglia's "Torn" begins to play, and for almost 15 seconds Armand looks straight ahead, expressionless, hands clasped in front of him. Then as the lyrics begin, Armand precisely mimes exaggerated, often comic, gestures for each word or phrase in the song. For example, the song begins with the phrase "Thought I saw a man come to life," so Armand points to his forehead for "thought," then to his eye for "I," and then from his eye out into the distance for the word "saw," all in the less than single second it takes for Imbruglia to sing those words.

The lyrics keep coming rapidly, and Armand keeps up, often making absurd cartoonlike faces or movements as he mimes phrases like, "he was dignified" (holding an imaginary monocle up to his eye and peering down at the audience over his nose), "showed me what it was to cry" (standing in a half crouch, rubbing both eyes, and opening his mouth wide in a mimed infant cry), and "into something real" (casting with an imaginary fishing pole and "reeling" it in as fast as possible), all the while staying right on the music. During breaks in the lyrics, Armand returns to staring straight ahead expressionless, arms down, hands clasped in front of him.

Throughout, we can hear laughter and cheers from the live audience. As the song begins to fade out at the end, Armand snaps to attention, feet together, hands clasped in front, and he bows crisply with mock seriousness from the waist. Then he turns and leaves the stage to enthusiastic applause, and the video fades to black. Overall, the video is 4 minutes and 41 seconds long, and it is one continuous shot with minimal camera movement.

A year later, Armand performed the same routine at the Secret Policeman's Ball fund-raiser for Amnesty International. Once again, several copies of the video were posted online, including *"Torn," by Johann Lippowitz with Natalie Imbruglia* (5.1 million views). This time however, it's a big multicamera TV production.

 "Torn," by Johann Lippowitz with Natalie Imbruglia

The song begins, and Armand goes through the same comic gestures, but about a minute and a half into the piece, the announcer's voice breaks in with, "Ladies and gentlemen… Miss Natalie Imbruglia!" and out onto the stage walks Natalie Imbruglia herself, singing live. We instantly realize that this entire time, Armand wasn't miming to a recording but to Imbruglia singing live from backstage. As Armand continues his absurd routine, Imbruglia plays it straight, singing with complete conviction as she watches him act out the words. But when the chorus kicks in for the final time, Imbruglia turns to face the audience and joins Armand in miming the lyrics. And she nails it. She isn't just following him. She knows all the moves, and she does them in perfect synch with him as she continues to sing. When Imbruglia first joins in, the audience breaks into spontaneous applause. As she continues and it becomes clear that she's not just going to mime a few words but is really going for it—and that she's matching Armand move for move—the applause grows into wild laughter and cheers. As the song finishes, Armand and Imbruglia clasp their hands in front of themselves and bow in unison to enthusiastic applause.

How *"Torn," by Johann Lippowitz with Natalie Imbruglia,* and *Dance Interpretation of "Torn," by David Armand* Score on the Four Rules

Be True: The first video, *Dance Interpretation of "Torn," by David Armand*, follows all our rules very well. Style-wise, it's almost identical to *Evolution of Dance*: a stage, a spotlight, a single camera, and one solo performer dancing in ordinary clothing. The second version with Natalie Imbruglia has lots of edits, two giant video screens behind the performers, and higher production values in general, so that hurts its authenticity. The cameras sometimes swoop and zoom dramatically, so the second video loses the pure "we are there" effect of the first. Here, the editing and camerawork distract us by activating the orienting response. And sometimes the video even cuts to a different camera midgesture, obscuring what Armand is doing.

On the other hand, the fact that we're watching a live performance with a live audience helps a lot to counteract the excessive production values. We hear the audience responding, just as we are, to a live, true event. So while both videos get points for that, the first video gets more points for keeping its production values from interfering.

Don't Waste My Time: The second video scores better here. In the first video, we don't even see Armand enter the stage until we're 24 seconds in, the music doesn't start until 0:44, and he doesn't begin to mime the lyrics until 0:55. After that, however, it's one continuous money shot. We do need a little bit of setup to understand that Armand is supposed to be an *"artiste"* about to give us a "serious" modern dance interpretation of Natalie Imbruglia's song, but all of that is accomplished seeing him stand, unmoving in his slightly odd attire with his deadpan look, during the 12 seconds between the time he cues the music and the time the lyrics begin. In fact, that's almost exactly how the second video begins, and that version wastes almost no time through the entire piece.

Be Unforgettable: Armand's performance is impressive. To start with, he did something different. A parody modern dance "interpretation" of a pop song is something we've never seen before, and he did it well. The contrast between his ridiculous mime and his overly serious persona is undeniably funny, and he does a great job of hitting every mark of his choreography so that every word and phrase is done exactly when the music calls for it. This is a great example of "owning it." The piece wouldn't be nearly as successful, indeed it probably wouldn't work at all, if Armand had been sloppy with his choreography. As his subsequent performances of other songs have shown, he is indeed the world's leading expert in this odd little niche of interpretive mime.

But the second version with Natalie Imbruglia takes "unforgettable" up a notch. The first big unforgettable addition comes when Imbruglia first appears and we realize it's actually Natalie Imbruglia herself. We never expected that. Then toward the end when she matches him move for move for move in perfect synch, we love it, and we love her for doing it. It's no surprise to us the audience began to cheer at that point. That moment was unforgettable.

Humanity: Like *Evolution of Dance*, Armand's simple version does a great job of showing humanity. Armand's unadorned presentation lets us see him playing as his wacky character, and we get to enjoy how much effort Armand put into mastering his goofy routine.

The second version also does a great job here, and Natalie Imbruglia's unaffected presence takes it up another notch. Seeing a major recording artist like Imbruglia come out and cheerfully join in the lampooning of her own work really makes a connection. The fact that she took the time to learn (and master) Armand's ridiculous choreography helps us see her as a real person with a sense of humor and an ability to laugh at herself. The high point of the piece, when Imbruglia joins Armand and they move identically, is reminiscent of our favorite moment in *Where the Hell Is Matt? 2008* when Matt Harding breaks from his own dance and joins in with the sari-wearing South Asian dancers in their dance. Something about seeing someone join in, in perfect synch, with someone else's dance creates an immediate human connection.

Music: Imbruglia's cover of "Torn" works not only for the lyrics but for the melody and arrangement as well. It's a great, catchy pop tune, and it carries us happily through the piece as we watch Armand's antics. It's an energetic pop song, and that's good for contagiousness.

What We Might Have Done Differently: The only thing we'd have done differently in the first video would have been to start it when the music begins, rather than with the first minute or so of introduction and stretching. The version with Natalie Imbruglia knocks it out of the park on everything but the camerawork, and we'd simplify, simplify, simplify. While we recognize that it was originally shot for television, so it necessarily had different priorities, if the goal is maximum contagiousness online, simpler would be better.

KONY 2012

What It Is: According to online video metrics company Visible Measures, this video, at almost 30 minutes long, reached 100 million views in just six days, faster than any other video to date. *Mashable*, *Gizmodo*, and others have labeled it "the most viral video of all time."

KONY 2012

Made by the activist group Invisible Children, Inc., *KONY 2012* promotes the charity's efforts to have Ugandan warlord Joseph Kony brought to justice.

The video begins with title cards saying:

NOTHING IS MORE POWERFUL THAN AN IDEA
WHOSE TIME HAS COME
WHOSE TIME IS NOW

It then cuts to a rapid series of flickering, grainy images, which go by so quickly that many are hard to perceive. We see lines and circles—some of them resembling the rings of Saturn—then there's a quick flash of a red triangular logo before things slow down with a few longer shots of the Earth as seen from space. A voiceover, from director Jason Russell, then begins:

> *Right now, there are more people on Facebook than there were on the planet 200 years ago. Humanity's greatest desire is to belong and connect. And now, we see each other. We hear each other. We share what we love, and it reminds us what we all have in common.*

The video accompanies this with shots of people hugging, several close-ups of the YouTube "share" button, and a few emotional clips from various online videos like *Thumbs Up for Rock and Roll!* (5.3 million views) and *29 Years Old and Hearing Myself for the 1st Time!* (13 million views). It then returns to a view of the Earth from space, before cutting to images from the Arab Spring and other newsclips. The voiceover continues:

> *And this connection is changing the way the world works. Governments are trying to keep up. And older generations are concerned. The game has new rules. The next 27 minutes are an experiment. But in order for it to work, you have to pay attention.*

Links to These Videos

After a brief black screen, a countdown clock appears, showing each hundredth of a second flying by: 27:15:45 ... 27:15:20 ... 27:14:95.... Then a quick montage of clips flashes by: the Earth, people running, the red triangular logo, rings of Saturn, shooting stars ... and fade to black.

This introduction is 1 minute and 53 seconds long, and it includes more shots than you can count without slowing down the video.

It continues with shots of Russell's son Gavin being born and shots of Gavin as a young boy, dancing, making a snow angel, and making home movies with his dad. The narration includes, "I want him to grow up in a better world than I did."

Just over three and a half minutes into the video, we see the first hint of what the video is ultimately about when Russell, speaking to an auditorium of people, says, "Who are you to end a war? I'm here to tell you: who are you not to?"

Close to the four-minute mark, the video introduces another boy, Jacob Acaye, from Uganda. We see him living in squalor, telling the story of seeing his brother killed by rebels, voicing fears of being abducted and killed, and crying as he thinks of what he would say to his brother if he could speak to him again. We hear Russell's voice from behind the camera, promising Jacob, "We are also going to do everything that we can to stop them."

At roughly nine minutes into the video, Russell first mentions Joseph Kony, the Lord's Resistance Army (the LRA), and the purpose of the video:

> If we succeed, we change the course of human history.... This movie expires on December 31, 2012. And its only purpose is to stop the rebel group, the LRA, and their leader Joseph Kony.

The rest of the video includes more montages of blisteringly fast shots of activists with fists upraised, helicopters, people putting up posters, the White House, African children dancing, people building with bricks, Hitler, Osama bin Laden, dead bodies, rows of skulls, people calling their senators, people writing letters,...

We see Russell telling his young son about "the bad guy," a reenactment of a child being violently dragged out of his bed, shots of the mutilated faces of children disfigured in the conflict, the International Criminal Court's list of "world's worst criminals" with Kony at the top of the list, and more. The allegations are horrific: murder, abduction, rape, and sexual slavery.

The voiceover moves to the steps being taken: "We rebuilt schools.... We created jobs.... And we built an early warning radio network." We see legislators speaking about the atrocities. We learn that American troops have been sent to advise in the hunt for Joseph Kony. We hear a group of kids chanting in unison about the effort to stop the atrocities against Ugandan children: "We've seen these kids. We've heard their cries. This war must end. We will not stop. We will not fear. We will fight war."

The video ends with an inspirational push to action, with images of the Earth, the recurring shot of planetary rings, the countdown clock going to zero, and young Gavin Russell saying, "I'm gonna be like you, Dad." The voiceover concludes with this:

> *We are not just studying human history. We are shaping it. At the end of my life, I want to say that the world we've left behind is one that Gavin can be proud of. . . . The better world we want is coming. It's just waiting for us to stop at nothing.*

Closing titles urge us to action:

1. SIGN THE PLEDGE
TO SHOW YOUR SUPPORT
2. GET THE BRACELET
AND THE ACTION KIT
3. SIGN UP FOR TRI TO DONATE
A FEW DOLLARS A MONTH
AND JOIN OUR ARMY
FOR PEACE
ABOVE ALL
SHARE THIS MOVIE ONLINE
IT'S FREE

This video has attracted a lot of controversy, both for its content and its style. Among other things, critics have argued that *KONY 2012* is years out of date since Joseph Kony and his forces left Uganda in 2006. They point out that while the video implies that the LRA is a large, powerful force, in fact it has now dwindled to less than a thousand members. In presenting its oversimplified picture of good versus evil, others note that the video ignores that Kony and the LRA are not alone in their atrocities in the region: the Ugandan Army and the Sudan People's Liberation Army, other military forces involved in the conflict, have also been accused of serious human rights abuses.

KONY 2012 has also been criticized for being manipulative, for focusing more on the story of director Jason Russell and his son Gavin than on Joseph Kony and the LRA, and for promoting a misguided neocolonialism.

Invisible Children claims that these flaws were unavoidable because in order to make a compelling video, the producers had to simplify the issues to present their message in a way that would motivate Western audiences.

How *KONY 2012* Scores on the Four Rules

As with many commercial projects, a significant part of the *KONY 2012* spread was not just organic word of mouth. This was a coordinated campaign with significant online support from heavy hitters. In the years preceding the release of *KONY 2012*, Invisible Children had cultivated a group of influential supporters who helped spread the word and generated views. Within the video itself, Invisible Children targeted 20 major celebrities with substantial online followings, including Oprah Winfrey, Lady Gaga, Justin Bieber, Ellen Degeneres, Mark Zuckerberg, Rihanna, George Clooney, Angelina Jolie, Taylor Swift, and Ryan Seacrest. Many of these celebrities, along with still others such as Bill Gates and Kim Kardashian, did indeed lend their efforts to help spread the video to millions. The *Guardian* reported that *KONY 2012* surged from 66,000 views to 9 million views simply after Oprah tweeted about it.

While unquestionably effective, this is not the same person-to-person, word-of-mouth viral spread our book is about. How much of *KONY 2012*'s success was due to the massive celebrity support it received and how much was due to viral qualities in the video itself is hard to know, but with that in mind, let's look at how *KONY 2012* scores on our four rules.

Be True: While the video has the ring of truth, as we mentioned above, the critics of *KONY 2012* raised concerns about how truthful it really is. That definitely harmed the contagiousness of the video: right or wrong, if you've heard that a video isn't truthful, the chances that you'll share it drop dramatically. While this is a real problem, the views here clearly outpaced the criticisms.

KONY 2012 also uses the heavy-handed editing and camera techniques of television, obscuring the truth. Only a few portions of the video are simple, uncut interviews with a handheld camera that capture a pure truth. Poor marks on this rule.

Don't Waste My Time: At almost 30 minutes long, this video is overloaded with time-wasting shots. It takes 9 minutes before we even find out who Joseph Kony is. And the video is completely centered on storytelling, from the story of Russell's son to the story of Jacob Acaye. Here too *KONY 2012* doesn't follow our rules.

Be Unforgettable: Here's where *KONY 2012* sets itself up for viral success. A 30-minute video about a Ugandan warlord, urging us to get involved—that's something different. It pushes to extremes of content, length, and style, making it a video that people talked about around the water cooler—truly unforgettable.

Humanity: This is a strength of *KONY 2012*'s, but it's played to the point of overkill. On PBS's *POV* documentary blog, Heather McIntosh wrote:

> *It attempts to go for the heart strings and not just tickle them but instead rip them out and stomp on them. The emotional appeals throughout this piece often overwhelm, and they run the risk of alienating a more questioning audience.*

Music: The piece also makes effective use of music to heighten emotional reactions throughout.

What We Might Have Done Differently: There are a lot of things we would do differently.

While *KONY 2012*'s sledgehammer approach has been effective in reaching millions, for many, including us personally, this approach made it hard to watch. The up-front manipulation immediately raised questions of credibility and made us withdraw rather than engage with it. Judy Barrass wrote on the *Critical Mass* blog, "I have to admit I didn't watch it all. At the risk of being howled down as insensitive and uncaring, I will say it was slow, boring, simplistic, and deliberately manipulative." Katie J. M. Baker at *Jezebel.com* had a similar reaction, writing, "The self-satisfied voiceover and slick editing reminded me of the most obnoxious Kickstarter-funded documentaries I've been asked to support." And *CityBeat*'s Ben Kaufman wrote that he found it "embarrassingly self-congratulatory."

For viewers like Barrass, Baker, Kaufman, and us, therefore, sharing it was out of the question.

More than anything, we would change the tone of this video to move away from a style that leaves some viewers feeling manipulated and toward a more direct approach that would honestly foster trust.

We would drastically simplify the editing and highlight the uninterrupted interviews, cut most of the nine-minute introductory narrative, and focus on the true emotions that are powerfully present in the content.

But while those changes would encourage more sharing, they would also sacrifice something. For example, there is a point to introducing Russell's son Gavin: as emotionally manipulative as it is, and as crass as it may sound to say it, Gavin gives Westerners someone to relate to more directly. On balance, it may do more harm than good, but it's undeniably powerful. And while including more information (such as making it clear that Kony is no longer in Uganda) would help the video be more truthful, the added complexity might interfere with the simple, contagious message: Joseph Kony is evil and must be stopped.

KONY 2012 also employs two mechanisms that fall outside our rules.

First, as Heather McIntosh pointed out in the *POV* blog, *KONY 2012* is propaganda. It has an agenda, and it pushes for it unapologetically. From the perspective of propaganda, the manipulative techniques can be useful. *KONY 2012* mixes active, positive emotions ("Who are you to end a war? I'm here to tell you: who are you not to?") with fear and shock (shots of disfigured children, Hitler, and rows of skulls). It's a compelling mix, and the emotion builds steadily. Unless the viewer starts questioning it and begins to resist, the propaganda techniques employed here create an effect we haven't seen in any other viral video.

Second, *KONY 2012* relies on another reason people share things. As social media expert David Vanderpoel has pointed out, one reason people share videos connected to a good cause is that the mere act of sharing itself makes them feel virtuous. As Vanderpoel put it, the video creates "a moral imperative to spread the word." *KONY 2012* pushes this kind of "slacktivism" hard, asserting repeatedly that if you will simply click "share," that act alone will make you an important part of the solution. Over and over, *KONY 2012* reinforces the notion that you will be a better person if you tell your friends about this video.

How replicable these techniques are remains to be seen. While it may be useful to tell your audience that the act of sharing your video is a good deed, and while it may be a repeatable mechanism for cause-related videos, for now *KONY 2012* stands alone as the only video to use such an unflinching arsenal of manipulative techniques to achieve viral success. As Matt Fiorentino of Visible Measures said (as quoted on *Mashable*), *KONY 2012* is "an anomaly."

[10]

Old Spice | The Man Your Man Could Smell Like

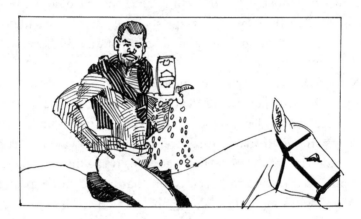

What It Is: This award-winning television commercial also became a crossover hit online, with 42 million views on YouTube, sequels like *Old Spice | Questions* (23 million views) and spoofs like *Sesame Street: Grover Stars in "Smell Like a Monster"* (9.6 million views).

The original 30-second spot begins looking like an ordinary television commercial. Clad only in a towel around his waist, former NFL player Isaiah Mustafa stands in a bathroom in front of a running shower. He looks directly into the camera and addresses himself not to the men usually targeted for men's grooming products, but to the women in the audience: "Hello, ladies," he says seductively. "Look at your man. Now back to me. Now back

The Man Your Man Could Smell Like

Links to These Examples

at your man. Now back to *me!*" As the camera moves in slowly, he continues, "Sadly, he isn't me—but if he stopped using lady-scented body wash and switched to Old Spice, he could smell like he's me."

Then the ad takes a fun, surreal turn. Never once looking away from the camera, Mustafa walks a few steps to his left and commands the viewers—or more precisely, the women in the audience—to "Look down. Now back up. Where are you? You're on a *boat*—with the man your man could smell like!" As he says this, the shower, sink, and bathroom in which he was standing fly up and out of frame, and Mustafa is now standing on the bow of a boat sailing on the open ocean. The towel around his waist falls away to reveal that he's wearing white jeans, and a shirt falls from above, landing casually around his shoulders. Unfazed, Mustafa continues to walk along the deck, keeping up his rapid-fire, tongue-in-cheek delivery. "What's in your hand?" he asks. "Back at me. I have it. It's an *oyster* with two tickets to that thing you *love.*" He lifts up his hand to show an oyster shell that opens to reveal two tickets inside. Almost as soon as they appear, the oyster and tickets turn to a pile of tiny diamonds that pour out of his hand as a bottle of Old Spice body wash rises up out of them. "The tickets are now *diamonds!*" says the bare-chested Mustafa. "*Anything* is possible when your man smells like Old Spice and not a lady… I'm on a *horse.*" As he says this final line, the camera pulls back, and we discover that Mustafa is indeed no longer on a boat at sea but is instead on a tropical beach sitting astride a white horse.

How *The Man Your Man Could Smell Like* Scores on the Four Rules

Be True: Although *The Man Your Man Could Smell Like* has many of the trappings of a traditional television commercial, which usually works against you online, it does a surprisingly good job at being true. On the one hand, this looks a lot like *Disneyland Musical*

Marriage Proposal: it's scripted, has perfect lights and sound, and Mustafa is exactly the kind of ideal-bodied, perfectly coiffed Hollywood actor that would typically ruin most viral efforts. But the very point of the ad is to make fun of precisely how much that flawless spokesmodel look contrasts with how the real people watching actually look and how much this fantasy world contrasts with ours.

Mustafa is both making his point for Old Spice and playing with us. He's showing off for us what the life of the ideal man like him is like: one moment he's home in the shower, the next he's on a yacht and diamonds are appearing in his hand, and then he's riding a horse down a tropical beach. And he does it in a way that shows he knows that we know it's clearly pretend.

Mustafa's direct, straight-to-the-camera delivery and the fact that he's clearly having fun with this send-up of a typical television commercial do a great job of creating an immediate connection with the audience. It seems as though he's really speaking directly to us and enjoying, with us, the absurdity of the fantasy he's pretending to sell.

In addition, part of what makes all of this work is that, like so many other successful online videos, *The Man Your Man Could Smell Like* is also shot in a single, uninterrupted take. Surprisingly, the only digital effect added after the shoot was the transformation of the oyster shell and tickets into the pile of diamonds out of which the Old Spice body wash appeared. Everything else was shot in real time as it actually happened.

The realistic bathroom set, complete with running shower, in which Mustafa first appears was specially designed so that it could be lifted away by a crane at exactly the right moment to reveal the boat set that was built behind it on a real beach. The boat set itself was shot from a low angle to hide the beach beneath it and make it appear as though the boat was actually sailing in the middle of the ocean. Then without breaking his direct gaze into the camera or missing the rhythm of his rapid-fire lines, Mustafa walked along the deck and settled himself onto a specially made saddlelike platform that was out of sight, just below the frame of the camera. Crew members then pulled the platform along on cables until it gently slid Mustafa right onto the back of the waiting white horse.

Getting everything to work perfectly took no less than 67 separate takes, but Mustafa and the team from Old Spice's agency, Wieden + Kennedy, knew that the piece had to be done in a single, unedited shot, so they kept at it until they got what they needed. The behind-the-scenes video taken during the shoot that shows how it all worked is well worth a look.

Don't Waste My Time: Not a second is wasted. From the moment the ad begins and Mustafa looks directly into the camera to address the "ladies" watching at home, we get nothing but money shot after money shot. It goes right from one clever scene change to another, with surprising costume changes and funny lines—all packed tightly into 30 seconds. There are no establishing shots to set the scene, and there is no time wasted on introducing Mustafa's "character." High marks here.

Be Unforgettable: This is where the video excels. Mustafa's mock-serious attitude, his cheeky but playful "look at me, ladies, and see how much more magnificent I am than your man" direct-to-the-camera message, and the impressive shower-to-boat-to-beach-to-horseback transformations all combine to make for a memorable, one-of-a-kind experience.

Humanity: As with Rule One, here too this piece goes against what we'd ordinarily recommend: a too-perfect actor looking down on all of us from a pedestal, but here it's all done in order to parody exactly that. We also get to see something of the real Isaiah Mustafa having some fun with his own hyperperfect male model image. He comes across as a real and likable guy.

Music: None but the traditional Old Spice jingle at the end, which was all it needed.

What We Might Have Done Differently: This highly produced piece works extremely well, walking a difficult line to find success both on TV and online. If we focus only on what would help make it more contagious online, two strengths emerge that could be built on: the direct address to the audience and the elaborate sequence of set changes. Just how crazy could those set changes get? Could we eliminate the need for that one digital effect? We would take this video more in the direction of OK Go's *This Too Shall Pass—Rube Goldberg Machine* or *LIPDUB: I Gotta Feeling (Comm-UQAM 2009)*, in which the sequence of events captured in one unbroken shot is mind-bogglingly elaborate and everything is undeniably real. We'd love to see what would happen if we mixed together the scale and truth of *This Too Shall Pass—Rube Goldberg Machine* with the concept and brash, playful attitude of *The Man Your Man Could Smell Like.*

Notes

All websites referenced were accessed June 2012.

Introduction

Page viii ▸ The estimated view count for *The Extreme Diet Coke & Mentos Experiments* is based on combined views of television appearances, existing online copies, and online copies that have been taken down.

Chapter 1: Everything You Know Is Wrong

Page 1 ▸ Tim Street quotation: Tim Street interview with Stephen Voltz, June 2012.

Page 3 ▸ Jonah Berger and Katherine Milkman on sharing: Jonah Berger and Katherine L. Milkman, "What Makes Online Content Viral?" *Journal of Marketing Research,* vol. 49, no. 2, April 2012, pp. 192–205.

Page 3 ▸ Robert Kubey and Mihaly Csikszentmihalyi on the effects of television: Robert Kubey and Mihaly Csikszentmihalyi, "Television Addiction Is No Mere Metaphor," *Scientific American,* February 2002.

Page 4 ▸ Annie Lang, and others, with research on the effects of edits: Annie Lang, Shuhua Zhou, Nancy Schwartz, Paul D. Bolls, and Robert F. Potter, "The Effects of Edits on Arousal, Attention, and Memory for Television Messages: When an Edit Is an Edit, Can an Edit Be Too Much?" *Journal of Broadcasting & Electronic Media,* Winter 2000. Available online at http://www.tandfonline.com/doi/abs/10.1207/s15506878jobem4401_7#preview.

Sidebar: A Word About View Counts

Page 6 ▸ Jimmy Kimmel's effect on *Double Rainbow,* explained in YouTube Trends Manager Kevin Allocca's TEDYouth talk: *Kevin Allocca: Why Videos Go Viral,* recorded November 2011, posted online February 2012. Available online at http://www.ted.com/talks/kevin_allocca_why_videos_go_viral.html.

Page 6 ▸ Multi-million-dollar ad buy behind *The Force*: Candace Lombardi, "VW partners with Lucasfilm for Super Bowl ad," *CNET Green Tech,* January

26, 2011. Available online at http://news.cnet.com/8301-11128_3-20029611-54.html.

Page 6 ▶ Ad buy behind *The Man Your Man Could Smell Like*: Wieden+Kennedy, *Case Study: Old Spice & Wieden+Kennedy, "The Man Your Man Could Smell Like,"* posted to YouTube on June 10, 2011. Available online at http://www.youtube.com/watch?v=iS-4WxmKBNI.

Page 6 ▶ Buying views for a video of watching paint dry: Jack Leonard and David Sarno, "Yes, Watching Paint Dry Can Fetch Plenty of Web Views," *Los Angeles Times*, March 3, 2012. Available online at http://articles. latimes.com/2012/mar/03/local/la-me-trutanich-video-20120304.

Rule One: Be True

Page 9 ▶ Todd Robbins quotation: In Tony Gangi, *Carny Sideshows: Weird Wonders of the Midway*, Citadel Press, New York, 2010, p. 48.

Chapter 3: Show Me Something Real

Page 14 ▶ Chris Brown's 2008 pop hit "Forever": *JK Wedding Entrance Dance* moved Chris Brown's year-old song "Forever" up to number 4 on iTunes and number 3 on Amazon. Oliver Chiang, "The Wedding Dance Crashers: How to Cash In on Viral Videos," *Forbes.com*, August 11, 2009. Available online at http://www.forbes.com/2009/08/11/indigo-productions-video-technology-e-gang-09-indigo.html.

Page 14 ▶ *JK Wedding Entrance Dance* uploaded: Jill Peterson and Kevin Heinz's wedding was on June 2, 2009, at Christ Lutheran Church in St. Paul. The video was not uploaded until July 19, 2009. One week later it had already received 10 million views. Greg McCoral, "JK Wedding Entrance Dance," *Know Your Meme*, Summer 2009, updated July 20, 2012. Available online at http://knowyourmeme.com/memes/jk-wedding-entrance-dance.

Page 15 ▶ *Disneyland Musical Marriage Proposal* was faked: Adam Townsend, "Disneyland Gets Viral with Elaborate Fake Marriage Proposal," *Orange County Register*, July 9, 2009. Available online at http://ocresort.ocregister.com/2009/07/09/disneyland-gets-viral-with-elaborate-fake-marriage-proposal/11519/.

Page 16 ▶ Rehearsal time for *JK Wedding Entrance Dance*: The wedding party in *JK Wedding Entrance Dance* rehearsed for only an hour and a half. Oliver Chiang, "The Wedding Dance Crashers: How to Cash In on Viral Videos," *Forbes.com*, August 11, 2009. Available online at http://www.forbes.com/2009/08/11/indigo-productions-video-technology-e-gang-09-indigo.html.

Chapter 4: Just Press Record and Do It

Page 21 ▶ Trish Sie quotation, "[You] want to stick to that original feeling of: if you were in the room, this is what it really looked like": Trish Sie interview with Madeleine Brand, *The Madeleine Brand Show*, KPCC Radio, October 1, 2010. Available online at http://www.scpr.org/programs/madeleine-brand/2010/10/01/16280/ok-go.

Page 23 ▶ Background on Judson Laipply and *Evolution of Dance*: Judson Laipply, "Judson Laipply, Inspirational Comedian and Evolution of Dance Creator," *Might as Well Dance*, http://www.mightaswelldance.com/biography/.

Page 25 ▶ *All Things Considered*, Robert Siegel quotation: "Of 'A Million Ways' to Be Popular, OK Go Finds One," *All Things Considered*, National Public Radio, August 30, 2005. Available online at http://www.npr.org/templates/story/story.php?storyId=4824604.

Page 25 ▶ Additional Trish Sie quotations: Trish Sie interview with Stephen Voltz, June 2012.

Page 25 ▶ Damian Kulash quotation: Damian Kulash interview with Robert Siegel, August 30, 2005, above.

Page 25 ▶ *Time* magazine's list of the all-time best music videos: OK Go's *Here It Goes Again* named one of *Time* magazine's top 30 music videos of all time. Claire Suddath, "The 30 All-TIME Best Music Videos: OK Go, 'Here It Goes Again,'" *Time.com,* July 28, 2011. Available online at http://entertainment.time.com/2011/07/28/the-30-all-time-best-music-videos/#ok-go-here-it-goes-again-2006.

Page 26 ▶ Story behind the making of *White Knuckles*: *Behind the Scenes of White Knuckles—The Beginnings*, posted on YouTube, October 6, 2010. Available online at http://www.youtube.com/watch?v=JCIDJy4Ijf8.

Page 27 ▶ Roland Sonnenberg quotation: Jesus Diaz, "New OK Go Video Awesome Video Is Full of Awesome Dogs," *Gizmodo*, September 20, 2010. Available online at http://gizmodo.com/5643044/new-ok-go-video-is-awesome-and-full-of-awesome-dogs.

Chapter 5: I Am the Camera. Take Me There.

Page 31 ▶ Background on the OK Go Rube Goldberg machine: Dylan Tweney, "How OK Go's Amazing Rube Goldberg Machine Was Built," *Wired Gadget Lab*, March 2, 2010. Available online at http://www.wired.com/gadgetlab/2010/03/ok-go-rube-goldberg/.

Page 32 ▶ Background on the making of the UQAM lipdub: Pierre-Etienne Caza, "The UQAM lipdub: behind the scenes," *Journal L'UQAM*, vol. 36, no. 3, October 5, 2009. Available online at http://www.uqam.ca/en/interviews/lipdub2009.htm.

Chapter 6: For Marketers: Be Honest

Page 38 ▶ AJ Brustein on the *Happiness Machine*: AJ Brustein interview with Meaghan Edelstein, "How Coca-Cola Created Its 'Happiness Machine,'" *Mashable*, July 21, 2010. Available online at http://mashable.com/2010/07/21/coke-happiness-machine/.

Page 40 ▶ *BusinessWeek* on *Wal-Marting Across America*: Pallavi Gogoi, "Wal-Mart's Jim and Laura: The Real Story," *Businessweek.com*, October 9, 2006. Available online at http://www.businessweek.com/stories/2006-10-09/wal-marts-jim-and-laura-the-real-storybusinessweek-business-news-stock-market-and-financial-advice.

Page 40 ▶ *CNN Money* on *Wal-Marting Across America*: Adam Horowitz, David Jacobson, Tom McNichol, and Owen Thomas, "101 Dumbest Moments in Business, #54," *CNN Money*. Available online at http://money.cnn.com/galleries/2007/biz2/0701/gallery.101dumbest_2007/54.html.

Page 40 ▶ The *Motley Fool* on Walmart's previous blogging "lies of omission": Alyce Lomax, "Wal-Mart's Blogging Blunder," *Motley Fool*, March 7, 2006. Available online at http://www.fool.com/investing/general/2006/03/07/walmarts-blogging-blunder.aspx#.T_NWde1WLao.

Page 40 ▶ The *New York Times* on anonymity: Brian Stelter, "Upending Anonymity: These Days the Web Unmasks Everyone," *New York Times*, June 20, 2011. Available online at http://www.nytimes.com/2011/06/21/us/21anonymity.html.

Page 41 ▶ John Grant on authenticity: John Grant, *The New Marketing Manifesto*, Thomson Texere, London, July 2000, p. 98.

Rule Two: Don't Waste My Time

Page 43 ▶ Natasha Veruschka quotation: In Tony Gangi, *Carny Sideshows: Weird Wonders of the Midway*, Citadel Press, New York, 2010, p. 147.

Chapter 8: Don't Tell Me a Story

Page 56 ▶ Randall Rothenberg and Mike Hughes on storytelling: Randall Rothenberg and Mike Hughes, "You Have All the Tools You Need to Build Better Brand Stories," *AdAge Blogs*, September 19, 2011. Available online at http://adage.com/article/guest-columnists/storytelling-apple-google-chevy-led-success/229814/.

Page 56 ▶ Chip Heath and Dan Heath on stories: Chip and Dan Heath, *Made to Stick*, Random House, New York, 2007, p. 18.

Page 56 ▶ *Time* magazine's *NewsFeed* on *Baby Monkey (Going Backwards on a Pig)*: Megan Gibson, "Video: Baby Monkey Riding a Baby Pig—Enough

Said," *Time NewsFeed*, September 17, 2010. Available online at http://newsfeed.time.com/2010/09/17/video-baby-monkey-riding-a-baby-pig-enough-said/.

Chapter 9: No #&$@ing Product Shots

Page 63 ▶ On omnipresent brand advertising: Louise Story, "Anywhere the Eye Can See, It's Likely to See an Ad," *New York Times*, January 15, 2007. Available online at http://www.nytimes.com/2007/01/15/business/media/15everywhere.html?ex=1326517200&en=02ff4c826cb60431&ei=5090&partner=rssuserland&emc=rss.

Page 67 ▶ Background on Cadbury's troubles in 2006: Jenny Wiggins, "The Inside Story of the Cadbury Takeover," *FT Magazine*, March 12, 2010. Available online at http://www.ft.com/intl/cms/s/2/1e5450d2-2be5-11df-8033-00144feabdc0.html#axzz1ljhQS52z.

Page 67 ▶ "2007. . . was the year of the gorilla": Simon Bowers, "Much Aped Chocolate Advert Scores with the Public," *Guardian*, February 19, 2008. Available online at http://www.guardian.co.uk/business/2008/feb/20/cadburyschweppesbusiness.fooddrinks.

Page 68 ▶ On the Blendtec sales increase: Xavier Lanier, "BlendTec CEO Says Sales up 700% Since Launching 'Will It Blend?'" Tom Dickson interview with Xavier Lanier, *Notebooks.com*, posted on YouTube, January 14, 2009. Available online at http://www.youtube.com/watch?v=u6t92m1gwTY.

Page 68 ▶ On the Cadbury sales increases: Maggie Urry, "Gorilla Drums up Sales for Cadbury," *Financial Times*, December 12, 2007. Available online at http://www.ft.com/intl/cms/s/0/eb518256-a854-11dc-9485-0000779fd2ac.html#axzz1cTguIwYo. (Link requires registration.) Also, Jenny Wiggins, "Cadbury Aims to Bring Back Some Fizz," *Financial Times*, February 20, 2008. Available online at http://www.ft.com/intl/cms/s/0/0dc4643e-df55-11dc-91d4-0000779fd2ac.html#axzz1ljhQS52z. (Link requires registration.)

Page 68 ▶ On the T-Mobile sales lift: "T-Mobile—Dance—Case Studies," *Unruly Media*, July 10, 2009. Available online at http://www.unrulymedia.com/case-studies/t-mobile-dance.html.

Page 68 ▶ On the sales spikes of Coke and Mentos: *The Extreme Diet Coke & Mentos Experiments* increased sales of two-liter bottles of Diet Coke by between 5 and 10 percent and sales of Mentos by 15 percent. Adam Penenberg, "What Happens When You Let Go," *Media*, April 24, 2007. Available online at http://www.mediapost.com/publications/article/59256/what-happens-when-you-let-go.html.

Rule Three: Be Unforgettable

Page 71 ▶ *Time* magazine's "YouTube's 50 Best Videos" from 2010: Available online at http://www.time.com/time/specials/packages/completelist/0,29569,1974961,00.html.

Page 72 ▶ The *Sun's* list of YouTube's top 10: Bella Battle, "Top 10 YouTube videos Ever," *Sun*, April 13, 2010. Available online at http://www.thesun.co.uk/sol/homepage/features/2929426/Top-10-YouTube-videos-ever.html?offset=8.

Page 73 ▶ Rebecca Black's *Friday* view count total: Derived from combining the 35 million views of the current primary copy on YouTube with the estimated 167 million views before the first copy was taken off YouTube. The latter number comes from Alexia Tsotsis, "Rebecca Black Pulls Infamous 'Friday' Video from YouTube," *TechCrunch*, June 16, 2011. Available online at http://techcrunch.com/2011/06/16/rebecca-black-friday-video-no-longer-available-on-youtube/.

Page 74 ▶ Background on *Thriller* prison yard video: "Inmate 'Thriller' Video Is Web Hit," Paul Alexander (Associated Press), *USA Today*, August 9, 2007. Available online at http://usatoday30.usatoday.com/news/topstories/2007-08-09-2069158024_x.htm.

Chapter 10: Do Something Different

Page 79 ▶ Background on *Guess That Stain*: Josh Lasser, "*Celebrity Apprentice* Loses Its Mind," *Zap2It*, April 5, 2009. Available online at http://blog.zap2it.com/ithappenedlastnight/2009/04/the-celebrity-apprentice-loses-its-mind.html.

Page 81 ▶ Casey Neistat's *Bike Lanes* as an example of a video that includes something unexpected, from YouTube Trends Manager Kevin Allocca's TEDYouth talk: *Kevin Allocca: Why Videos Go Viral*, recorded November 2011, posted February 2012. Available online at http://www.ted.com/talks/kevin_allocca_why_videos_go_viral.html.

Page 81 ▶ Riding outside of the bike lanes in New York City is not illegal: John Del Signore, "Cyclist Ticketed for Riding Outside Bike Lane Fights Fine in State Supreme Court," *Gothamist*, March 6, 2012. Available online at http://gothamist.com/2012/03/06/cyclist_ticketed_for_biking_outside.php.

Chapter 11: Own It

Page 84 ▶ Background on Danny MacAskill: Carol Wallace, "A Stunt Cyclist's Tour de Fence," *New York Times*, December 28, 2009. Available online at

http://www.nytimes.com/2009/12/29/sports/global/29cyclist
.html?pagewanted=all.

Page 84 ▸ Background on Matt McAllister's T-shirt record: Brett Leigh Dicks,
"World Record," *Santa Barbara Independent*, October 26, 2006. Available online at http://www.independent.com/news/2006/oct/26/
world-record/.

Page 85 ▸ Matt McAllister's dangerous 2009 attempt: "KNIX's Matt McAllister Falls
Short of World Record," All Access Music Group, *Net News*, September
15, 2009. Available online at http://www.allaccess.com/net-news/
archive/story/63928/knix-s-matt-mcallister-falls-short-of-world-record.

Chapter 12: Capture a Unique Moment

Page 92 ▸ Charlie Todd quotation: Charlie Todd, interview with Stephen Voltz,
June 2012.

Page 93 ▸ Allen Funt's Army Signal Corps/Armed Forces Radio comedy work with
hidden microphones: Joe Teutonico, "'Smile, You're on Candid Camera'
Originator Allen Funt's B-Day," *Bensonhurst Bean*, September 16, 2011.
Available online at http://www.bensonhurstbean.com/2011/09/smile-
youre-on-candid-camera-originator-allen-funts-b-day/.

Page 94 ▸ Allen Funt's "early *Candid Microphone* stunts": "Candid Microphone,"
Old Time Radio Catalog. Available online at http://www.otrcat.com/
candid-microphone-p-2043.html.

Page 95 ▸ Allen Funt's goal "to catch people in the act of being themselves":
Tom Maurstad, "Smile. It's Been Half a Century Since Allen
Funt's First Victim," *Dallas Morning News*, August 29, 1996.
Available online at http://articles.sun-sentinel.com/1996-08-29/
lifestyle/9608270329_1_candid-camera-funt-s-son-allen-funt.

Rule Four: Ultimately, It's All About Humanity

Page 105 ▸ The Penn Jillette quotation: Penn Jillette, foreword to Drew Friedman,
Drew Friedman's Sideshow Freaks, Blast Books, New York, 2011,
pp. 10–11.

Chapter 14: Give Me the Thrill of Victory and the Agony of Defeat

Page 116 ▸ Research on the contagiousness of emotion: E. Hatfield, J. L. Cacioppo,
and R. L. Rapson, "Emotional Contagion," *Current Directions in
Psychological Sciences*, vol. 2, 1993, pp. 96–99. Available online at
http://www.elainehatfield.com/ch50.pdf.

Page 118 ▶ Background on Vinko Bagataj: Brent Musburger, "ABC Wide World Classic 'The Agony of Defeat' Vinko Bogataj Interview." Available online at http://www.youtube.com/watch?v=n_ZvwIFbXMM.

Page 119 ▶ Background on *Grape Lady Falls!*: Brad Kim, "Grape Lady: Part of a Series on FAIL," *Know Your Meme*. Available online at http://knowyourmeme.com/memes/grape-lady.

Sidebar: So Why Don't You Just Throw Your Arms Up in the Air and Skip All That Geyser Stuff?

Page 121 ▶ Throwing one's arms up in the air is a universal, hard-wired gesture of success and pride: Jessica Tracy and David Matsumoto, "The Spontaneous Expression of Pride and Shame: Evidence for Biologically Innate Nonverbal Displays," *Proceedings of the National Academy of Sciences*, 2008. Available online at http://www.pnas.org/content/105/33/11655.

Chapter 15: Show Humanity, Not Perfection

Page 124 ▶ The *New York Times* on *Numa Numa*: Alan Feuer and Jason George, "Internet Fame Is Cruel Mistress for a Dancer of the Numa Numa," *New York Times*, February 26, 2005. Available online at http://www.nytimes.com/2005/02/26/nyregion/26video.html.

Page 124 ▶ BBC News, citing the *Viral Factory*, puts views of *Numa Numa* at 700 million as of November 2006. How this number was reached is uncertain. See: "Star Wars Kid Is Top Viral Video," *BBC News*, November 27, 2006. Available online at http://news.bbc.co.uk/2/hi/entertainment/6187554.stm.

Page 124 ▶ Douglas Wolk on *Numa Numa*: Douglas Wolk, "The Syncher, Not the Song," *Believer*, June/July 2006. Available online at http://believermag.com/issues/200606/?read=article_wolk.

Page 126 ▶ The story of how Matt Harding decided to make *Where the Hell Is Matt?* (2008): Matt Harding interview with Stephen Voltz, June 2012.

Page 128 ▶ NPR, Robert Siegel quotation: "Of 'A Million Ways' to Be Popular, OK Go Finds One," *All Things Considered*, National Public Radio, August 30, 2005. Available online at http://www.npr.org/templates/story/story.php?storyId=4824604.

Page 128 ▶ Trish Sie quotation: Trish Sie interview with Stephen Voltz, June 2012.

Chapter 16: For Marketers: Let Your Brand Be Human

Page 134 ▶ The *Wall Street Journal* on Coke and Mentos: Suzanne Vranica and Chad Terhune, "Mixing Diet Coke and Mentos Makes a Gusher of

Publicity," *Wall Street Journal*, June 12, 2006. Available online at http://online.wsj.com/article/SB115007602216777497.html.

Page 134 ▸ The *Motley Fool* on Coke and Mentos: Rich Smith, "Coke Is an Idiot," *Motley Fool*, June 12, 2006. Available online at http://www.fool.com/investing/value/2006/06/12/coke-is-an-idiot.aspx#.T_N5-e1WLao.

Your Secret Weapon: Music

Page 139 ▸ Aristotle on music: Herman Helmholtz, *On the Sensations of Tone as a Physiological Basis for the Theory of Music*, 2nd English edition, Dover, New York, 1954 (originally published 1863), p. 251. In *Music and Emotion: Theory and Research*, edited by Patrik Juslin and John Sloboda, Oxford University Press, Oxford, U.K., 2001.

Page 139 ▸ Steven Pinker on music: Steven Pinker, *How the Mind Works*, Norton, New York, 1997, p. 528.

Page 139 ▸ Daniel Levitin on music: Daniel Levitin, *This Is Your Brain on Music*, Plume, New York, 2006, p. 191.

Page 143 ▸ Tim Street quotation: Tim Street interview with Stephen Voltz, June 2012.

Case Study 6: Lachen in der U-Bahn (Laughing in the Subway)

Page 174 ▸ Background on *Lachen in der U-Bahn*: "Lachen in der U-Bahn—der youtube-Hit," lachenverbindet. Available online at http://www.lachen-verbindet.de/index.php?option=com_content&view=article&id=85:lachen-in-der-u-bahn-der-youtube-hit-&catid=37:lachyoga&Itemid=58. (Web page is in German.)

Case Study 9: KONY 2012

Page 188 ▸ *Visible Measures* on *KONY 2012*: "Update: Kony Social Video Campaign Tops 100 Million Views," *Visible Measures Blog*, March 12, 2012. Available online at http://corp.visiblemeasures.com/news-and-events/blog/bid/79626/Update-Kony-Social-Video-Campaign-Tops-100-Million-Views.

Page 188 ▸ This was then referenced in: Todd Wasserman, "'KONY 2012' Tops 100 Million Views, Becomes the Most Viral Video in History," *Mashable*, March 12, 2012. Available online at http://mashable.com/2012/03/12/kony-most-viral/. Also, Mario Aguilar, "Kony 2012 Is the 'Most Viral' Video of All Time," *Gizmodo*, March 12, 2012. Available online at http://gizmodo.com/kony-2012/.

Page 191 ▶ A summary of many of the criticisms of *KONY 2012* and Invisible Children, Inc., as well as some of Invisible Children's rebuttals, can be found at: "Joseph Kony 2012 Video: 'Stop Kony' Campaign Draws Criticism," *Huffington Post*, March 8, 2012. Available online at http://www.huffingtonpost.com/2012/03/08/joseph-kony-video-stop-kony_n_1332427.html#s760454.

Page 193 ▶ Quotations about *KONY 2012*: Heather McIntosh, "KONY 2012: Analyzing the Viral Documentary Video," Public Broadcasting System's *POV* blog, March 10, 2012. Available online at http://www.pbs.org/pov/blog/2012/03/kony-2012-analyzing-the-viral-documentary-video/. See Judy Barrass, "Social Media as Manipulation: Kony 2012,"*Critical Mass* blog, March 9, 2012. Available online at http://www.criticalmassblog.net/?p=3900. See Katie J. M. Baker, "Think Twice Before Donating to Kony 2012, the Charitable Meme du Jour," *Jezebel,* March 7, 2012. Available online at http://jezebel.com/5891269/think-twice-before-donating-to-kony-2012-the-meme-du-jour. See Ben Kaufman, "Kony Video Is Manipulative But Effective," *CityBeat*, March 21, 2012. Available online at http://www.citybeat.com/cincinnati/article-25144-kony_video_is_manipulative_but_effective.html.

Page 195 ▶ David Vanderpoel quotation: David Vanderpoel interview with the authors, June 2012.

Page 195 ▶ *KONY 2012* is "an anomaly": Todd Wassermann, "KONY Sequel Got 2% of the Traffic of Its Predecessor," *Mashable,* April 16, 2012. Available online at http://mashable.com/2012/04/16/kony-sequel-traffic/.

Case Study 10: Old Spice | The Man Your Man Could Smell Like

Page 198 ▶ All shot in a single take: Liz Shannon Miller, "The Viral Genius of Wieden+Kennedy's New Old Spice Campaign," *Gigaom New Tee Vee.* Available online at http://gigaom.com/video/the-viral-genius-of-wiedenkennedys-new-old-spice-campaign/.

Page 199 ▶ Behind-the-scenes video: *The Man Your Man Could Smell Like: Behind the Scenes,* posted on YouTube, March 10, 2010. Available online at http://www.youtube.com/watch?v=ux4C-uC4mEg.

Page 199 ▶ A more complete description of the process of shooting the spot: Leo Laporte's 2010 interview with Wieden+Kennedy's Craig Allen and Eric Kallman in "TWiT Specials: The Making of Old Spice's Commercial: The Man Your Man Could Smell Like," *This Week in Technology TWiT TV.* Video of that interview, however, is no longer online.

List of Videos

The view counts for all videos are as of June 2012. You can find links to all these videos by following the QR Codes throughout this book or by visiting ViralVideoManifesto.com.

Title	Year	Views
29 Years Old and Hearing Myself for the 1st Time!	2011	13,000,000
Ark Hotel Construction Time Lapse Building 15 Storeys in 2 Days (48 Hours)	2010	5,600,000
Ask a Ninja [over 170 episodes]	2005–	Up to 5,000,000 each
Baby Monkey (Going Backwards on a Pig)— Parry Gripp	2010	14,000,000
Battle at Kruger	2007	67,000,000
Battle of the Year | 1 on 1 Bboy Battle	2010	5,200,000
Ben Takes a Photo of Himself Every Day	2006	2,900,000
Best Ever!!! (Kicesie Drew, the "Sexpert" Girl)	2007	150,000,000
The Best Surprise Military Homecomings: Part 1	2010	6,300,000
Bike Lanes by Casey Neistat	2011	5,600,000
Blue Streek 022012	2012	69,000
Breakdance—Hip Hop Battle	2006	9,600,000
Britain's Got Talent or America's Got Talent Connie Talbot WOWs Simon Cowell!	2007	120,000,000
Cadbury Dairy Milk: Airport Trucks Advert	2008	360,000
Cadbury Eyebrows (Official Version)	2009	9,300,000
Cadbury's Gorilla Advert August 31, 2007	2007	6,700,000
Charlie Bit My Finger—Again!	2007	460,000,000

Title	Year	Views
Charlie Schmidt's Keyboard Cat! —THE ORIGINAL!	2007	25,000,000
"Chocolate Rain" Original Song by Tay Zonday	2007	81,000,000
Christian the Lion	2008	18,000,000
Coca-Cola Happiness Machine	2010	4,800,000
Cute Puppy Falling Asleep. Golden Retriever Puppy.	2008	16,000,000
Daft Bodies: Harder, Better, Faster, Stronger	2007	16,000,000
Daft Hands: Harder, Better, Faster, Stronger	2007	54,000,000
Daft Hands: Technologic	2007	8,200,000
Dance Interpretation of "Torn" by David Armand	2006	950,000
Dancing Baby	1996	Unknown
Dancing Banana	2002	Unknown
Danny MacAskill, "Way Back Home"	2010	21,000,000
Dave Matthews Band, Everyday [originally released 2001]	2009	1,100,000
David After Dentist	2009	110,000,000
Did You Know?	2008	15,000,000
Disneyland Musical Marriage Proposal	2009	5,100,000
Dr. Horrible's Sing-Along Blog [released on Hulu]	2008	Unknown*
Dove Evolution	2006	15,000,000
Dramatic Chipmunk	2007	36,000,000
A Dramatic Surprise on a Quiet Square	2012	36,000,000
Dude Transports 22 Bricks on His Head	2008	1,900,000
Embrace Life: Always Wear Your Seat Belt	2010	15,000,000
Everest Elevator (Rémi Gaillard)	2011	4,100,000
Evolution of Dance, by Judson Laipply	2006	200,000,000
The Extreme Diet Coke & Mentos Experiments	2006	40,000,000
The Extreme Diet Coke & Mentos Experiments II— The Domino Effect	2006	10,000,000
The Extreme Sticky Note Experiments	2008	4,000,000
FAIL Blog: Roman Candle Headshot FAIL	2011	560,000
Foot Elevator (Rémi Gaillard)	2012	5,500,000
The Force: Volkswagen Commercial	2011	54,000,000
Free Hugs Campaign: Official Page, music by Sick Puppies	2006	73,000,000

Title	Year	Views
French Maid TV [13 episodes]	2006–	Up to 7,000,000 each
Friday—Rebecca Black—Official Music Video	2011	200,000,000
Frustrated Skateboarder Fail	2009	4,300,000
Funny Cats	2006	17,000,000
Fuzzy Fuzzy Cute Cute—Parry Gripp	2009	6,400,000
Grape Lady Falls!	2007	12,000,000
Greatest Marriage Proposal Ever!!!	2011	23,000,000
Greyson Chance Singing Paparazzi	2010	48,000,000
Guess That Stain	2009	2,600
Guinness World Record for Most T-Shirts Worn at One Time	2006	17,000,000
Guys Backflip into Jeans	2008	8,000,000
Hitler's Downfall	2006	Unknown
Improv Everywhere: Frozen Grand Central	2008	31,000,000
Improv Everywhere: No Pants Subway Ride 2009	2009	19,000,000
Inspired Bicycles, Danny MacAskill, April 2009	2009	31,000,000
Jamin's Downtown Disney Proposal	2011	5,800,000
Jason McElwain Autistic Basketball Player	2006	2,800,000
JK Divorce Dance	2009	9,900,000
JK Wedding Entrance Dance	2009	76,000,000
Karaoke for the Deaf	2005	520,000
KONY 2012	2012	92,000,000
Lachen in der U-Bahn, www.lachen-verbindet.de	2011	3,200,000
Laker Kobe Bryant Attempts Massive Stunt… and Succeeds! Real?	2008	5,200,000
The Landlord	2007	79,000,000
Laughing Baby	2006	5,800,000
Leave Britney Alone!	2007	44,000,000
LIPDUB: I Gotta Feeling (Comm-UQAM 2009)	2009	10,000,000
The Little Girl Giant	2006	3,100,000
Me: Girl Takes Pic of Herself Every Day for Three Years	2006	9,000,000
MEGAWOOSH—Bruno Kammerl Jumps	2009	6,200,000

Title	Year	Views
Mister Universe (Rémi Gaillard)	2008	25,000,000
おサルのロデオ *(Monkey Rodeo Movie)*	2010	680,000
My Drunk Kitchen [over 25 episodes]	2011–	Up to 1,900,000 each
Natalie Time Lapse: Birth to 10 Years Old in 1 Minute 25 Seconds	2008	7,300,000
Noah Takes a Photo of Himself Every Day for Six Years	2006	23,000,000
Nom Nom Nom Nom Nom Nom Nom—Parry Gripp	2009	19,000,000
Numa Numa	2004	Est. 700,000,000
The Office: The Accountants	2006	Unknown*
OK Go—A Million Ways	2005	1,500,000
OK Go—Here It Goes Again (treadmills)	2006	66,000,000
OK Go—This Too Shall Pass, Rube Goldberg Machine Version	2010	36,000,000
OK Go—White Knuckles, Official Video (OK Go—Dogs)	2010	14,000,000
*Old Spice	Questions*	2010	23,000,000
*Old Spice	The Man Your Man Could Smell Like*	2010	42,000,000
One on One Breakdance Battle—Red Bull BC One Cypher 2012 Bulgaria	2012	35,000
The Page Turner	2011	6,700,000
Paul Potts Sings "Nessun Dorma"	2007	96,000,000
Photo Booth Pranks [The Tonight Show]	2012	2,800,000
Porcupine Who Thinks He Is a Puppy!	2009	2,800,000
Puppy Versus Cat	2006	14,000,000
RickRoll'D	2007	63,000,000
Rob Dyrdek on a Floating Skateboard????	2011	660,000
Sand Art by Ilana Yahav, SandFantasy, "You've Got a Friend"	2008	4,300,000
Sarah Palin, Tina Fey on Saturday Night Live	2008	12,000,000
Scooter Handling FAIL	2010	2,800,000
Selyna Bogino Doing the Five Balls Longest Routine Ever! XD	2011	1,600,000
Selyna Bogino—Tigerpalast 2011	2011	44,000

Title	Year	Views
Sesame Street: Grover Stars in "Smell Like a Monster"	2010	9,600,000
Skateboarding Dog	2007	20,000,000
The Sneezing Baby Panda	2006	140,000,000
Soldier Homecoming Surprise Mix	2010	9,800,00
Sony Bravia: Bouncy Balls	2006	4,900,000
Sony Bravia: Colours—Pyramids TV Advert	2007	330,000
Sony Bravia: Domino City	2008	480,000
Sony Bravia: Paint Ad	2006	1,500,000
Sony Bravia: Play-Doh	2007	1,600,000
Star Wars Kid	2003	26,000,000
Star Wars: The Phantom Menace Review	2009	4,100,000
The Sultan's Elephant	2006	390,000
Susan Boyle: Britain's Got Talent 2009 Episode 1, Saturday 11th April / HD High Quality	2009	96,000,000
"Thriller" (original upload)	2007	51,000,000
Thumbs Up for Rock and Roll!	2011	5,300,000
Tiger Woods Nike Golf Commercial [originally aired in 1999]	2007	1,900,000
The T-Mobile Dance	2009	35,000,000
The T-Mobile Royal Wedding	2011	26,000,000
The T-Mobile Welcome Back	2010	12,000,000
"Torn," by Johann Lippowitz with Natalie Imbruglia	2006	5,100,000
Unbelievable David Beckham Three Balls into a Trash Can!!	2011	1,200,000
University of Florida Student Tasered at Kerry Forum [a.k.a. Don't Tase Me, Bro!]	2007	6,500,000
Walk on Water, Liquid Mountaineering	2010	12,000,000
The Way Things Go	2009	210,000
We No Speak Americano ft. Cleary & Harding	2010	8,800,000
Web Therapy	2008–	Unknown*
What News Anchors Do During Commercial Breaks, with Sound	2009	3,000,000
Where the Hell Is Matt? 2006	2006	18,000,000
Where the Hell Is Matt? 2008	2008	43,000,000

Title	Year	Views
Will It Blend? [over 110 episodes]	2006–	200,000,000 total views
Will It Blend?—Glow Sticks	2007	9,300,000
Will It Blend?—Golf Balls	2006	7,000,000
Will It Blend?—Hockey Pucks	2006	2,600,000
Will It Blend?—iPad	2010	14,000,000
Will It Blend?—iPhone	2007	11,000,000
Will It Blend?—Justin Bieber	2011	1,900,000
Will It Blend?—Marbles	2006	5,900,000
Yosemitebear Mountain Giant Double Rainbow 1-8-10	2010	34,000,000

*Most views occurred off YouTube and are hard to measure.

Acknowledgments

We'd especially like to thank Michael Miclon and John Voltz for seeing the potential for this book and for urging us repeatedly to sit down and write it. Without their encouragement, we probably never would have even started this project.

We'd also like to thank all of our friends, colleagues, and fellow viral video creators who have been so generous with their time—either in reviewing early drafts, sharing their ideas, or both—particularly:

Julia Brotherton
Greg Cohen
Dan Fukushima
Stephanie Frerich
Stafford Green
Charles and Elizabeth Grobe
Matt Harding
Judson Laipply
Kent Nichols
Christopher Peterson
Stephanie Kip Rostan
Trish Sie
Tim Street
Meghan Strell
Charlie Todd
Casey Turner
David Vanderpoel
and
Cindy Voltz

Index

Note: Page numbers in *italic* refer to illustrations and QR hyperlinks.

About the Authors

Stephen Voltz and **Fritz Grobe** are the creators of the viral video studio EepyBird.

From their first online video featuring the explosive combination of Coke and Mentos that *Advertising Age* called the most important commercial content of the year to their viral campaigns for brands including OfficeMax, Coca-Cola, and ABC Family, EepyBird's videos have been seen over 150 million times. EepyBird has received four Webby Awards and two Emmy nominations, and it was voted "Game Changer of the Decade" on GoViral.com.

Stephen and Fritz have appeared on the *Late Show with David Letterman, Ellen, The Today Show, Mythbusters,* and more. They have performed in Las Vegas, New York, Paris, London, and Istanbul.

They come by their rigorously analytic approach to Internet video honestly. Stephen has a law degree from NYU and practiced as a trial lawyer in Boston for 20 years. Fritz studied mathematics at Yale University until he dropped out of school to become an award-winning circus performer.